King of the Jews
A story of Christ's last days on Earth

W. T. Stead

King of the Jews: A story of Christ's last days on Earth

Copyright © 2022 Indo-European Publishing

All rights reserved

The present edition is a reproduction of previous publication of this classic work. Minor typographical errors may have been corrected without note; however, for an authentic reading experience the spelling, punctuation, and capitalization have been retained from the original text.

ISBN: 978-1-64439-633-9

CONTENTS

I	JESUS DRIVES OUT MONEY CHANGERS	1
II	JESUS' LAST JOURNEY TO JERUSALEM	13
III	THE LAST SUPPER	29
IV	BETRAYED BY A KISS	44
V	PETER COMMITS PERJURY	58
VI	JUDAS HANGS HIMSELF	69
VII	JESUS, PILATE AND HEROD	77
VIII	"JESUS OR BARABBAS"	90
IX	THE CRUCIFIXION	104
X	CONCLUSION	125

CHAPTER I

JESUS DRIVES OUT THE MONEY-CHANGERS

> Cast thyself down in adoring love,
> Race bowed down by the curse of God!
> Peace and grace out of Zion above!
> He is not wroth forever,
> Though his wrath be just—though uplifted his rod.
> Thus saith he, who changeth never:
> "I will not the death of a sinner—I will forgive—
> Let him live!"
> And he gave up his son the world from sin to free,
> Praise and thanks we give, Eternal, to thee!

Suddenly there was heard a noise of singing. A great multitude came pouring down the narrow street that runs past Pilate's house, chanting as they came, "Hail to thee, O Son of David!" Little children, old men and maidens ran forward, some raising palm branches, but all ever looking backward to one who should come. More and ever more streamed down the street into the open space in front of the temple, but still the Hosanna song went on.

At last, in the midst of the jubilant throng, Jesus appeared, clad in a long garment of gray, over which was cast a flowing robe. His face was composed and pensive. His long black hair and beard surrounded features somewhat swarthy from the rays of the hot sun, and he rode on the side of the ass's colt that seemed almost too small to support his weight.

John, the beloved disciple, dressed in green raiment with a red mantle, led the little ass, carrying in his hand a long pilgrim staff. The mob pressed tumultuously around, singing and crying: "Hosanna to the Son of David!" Jesus blessed them as he rode through their midst. After passing the house of Pilate he suddenly dismounted. Then Jesus advanced to the front of the temple. The hosannas died away as he contemplated the busy scene. There were the priests busily engaged with the money-changers. Nathanael, chief orator of the Sanhedrin, stood conspicuous among the chattering throng. There were baskets with pigeons for sale as sacrifices. There were the tables of the dealers. Buying and selling, haggling and bargaining were in full swing in the market-place.

For a moment Jesus, who was above the average height, and whose mien was dignified and commanding, stood as if amazed and indignant, then suddenly burst out upon the astonished throng of priests and merchants, with the following protest: "What see I here? Shall my Father's house be thus dishonored? Is this the house of God, or is it a market-place? How can the strangers who come from the land of the Gentiles to worship God perform their devotions in this tumult of usury? And you," he continued, advancing a step toward the priests, who stared at him in amazement, "You priests, guardians of the temple, can you see this abomination and permit it to continue? Woe be unto you! He who searches the heart knows why you encourage such disorder."

The crowd, silent now, watched with eager interest the money-changers and priests, who but imperfectly understanding what had been said to them, stared at the intruder.

"Who can this man be?" they asked.

And then from the lips of all the multitude there went up the simultaneous response, as if the whole throng had but one voice: "It is the great prophet from Nazareth, in Galilee!"

Jesus, then moving forward into the midst of the astonished merchants in the temple, exclaimed, in words of imperious authority: "Away with you from here, servants to Mammon! I command it. Take what belongs to you and quit the holy place!"

One of the traders exclaimed in terror: "Come, let us go, that his wrath destroy us not."

Then the priests, recovering somewhat their self-possession, stepped forward to remonstrate. "Why troublest thou this people?" they asked. "Everything here is for sacrifice. How canst thou forbid that which the council has allowed?" And then the traders, led by one Dathan, chimed in, in eager chorus: "Must there then be no more sacrifices?"

For answer Jesus stood forth and exclaimed: "There is room enough outside the temple for your business. 'My house,' says the Lord, 'shall be called a house of prayer for all nations;' you have made it a den of thieves."

And then crying, "Away with all this!" with one vigorous movement he overturned the tables of the money-changers.

A rabbi exclaimed: "This must not be—thou darest not do this!" but his voice passed unheeded in the tumult. The earthenware vessels fell crashing to the ground, the money was scattered over the floor. Some of the dismayed merchants crying, "My money, oh! my money," scrambled for the glittering coins. Others stared in fury at the unceremonious intruder. Half a dozen doves, released from their wicker baskets, took to flight amid the despairing lamentation of their owners: "Oh, my doves; who will compensate me for this loss?"

Their lamentations were rudely cut short. A small rope was hanging near by. Seizing it in the middle and twisting it once or twice round his hand, Jesus converted it into a whip of cords, with which he drove out the traders. "Away! get you hence. I will that this desecrated place be restored to the worship of the Father!"

The traders fled, but the priests remained, and, after muttering together, they asked in angry tones: "By what miraculous sign dost thou prove that thou hast the power to act in this wise?"

Jesus answered them: "You seek after a sign; yea, a sign shall be given unto you. Destroy this temple, and in three days I will have built it up again."

The priests replied, contempt mingling with indignation in their tones: "What a boastful declaration! Six and forty years was this temple in building, and thou wilt build it up again in three days!"

At this point the children who had been standing around watching the altercation with the dealers, cried out in unison with their elders: "Blessed be he that cometh in the name of the Lord!"

The priests, shocked at their homage, were sorely displeased, and appealed to Jesus, saying: "Hearest thou what they say? Forbid them!"

They paused for his reply.

Then Jesus answered and said unto them: "I say unto you, if they were silent the very stones would cry out."

Encouraged by this emphatic approval, the children cried out once more, louder than ever, the sound of their childish voices filling the temple: "Hosanna to the Son of David!"

Then the Pharisees, who stood by the overthrown tables of the money-changers, spoke up and said angrily to the little ones: "Silence, you silly children!"

Jesus turned to them and said: "Have you never read 'Out of the mouths of babes and sucklings thou hast perfected praise.' That which is hidden from the proud is revealed unto babes?" And as the priests and Pharisees muttered in indignation among themselves, he continued: "For the Scripture must be fulfilled. The stone which the builders rejected is become the headstone of the corner. The Kingdom of God shall be taken from you and it shall be given to a people which shall bring forth the fruits thereof. But that stone, whosoever shall fall upon it shall be broken, but on whomsoever it shall fall it shall grind him to powder. Come, my disciples, I have done what the Father has commanded me, I have vindicated the honor of his house. The darkness remains darkness, but in many hearts it will soon be day. Let us go into the inner court of the temple that we may there pray unto the Father." Thereupon Jesus, followed by his disciples, disappeared in the interior of the temple, while the people cried aloud as with one voice: "Praise be to the anointed one!" and the priests said angrily: "Silence, rabble!" The Pharisees adding: "Ye shall all be overthrown with your leader." To which the crowd responded by crying louder than ever: "Blessed be the Kingdom of David which again appears!"

Then Nathanael, a leading man in the Sanhedrin, tall and well favored, wearing a horned mitre, and possessing the tongue of an orator, stood forth, and seeing Jesus had departed and that there was now no one to withstand him in the hearing of the people, lifted up his voice and cried: "Whosoever holds with our fathers Abraham, Isaac and Jacob, let him stand by us! The curse of Moses upon all the rest!"

Then a rabbi in blue velvet apparel, sprang forward and declared with a loud voice: "He is a deceiver of the people, an enemy of Moses, an enemy of the Holy Law!" The people answered mockingly: "Then, if so, why did you not arrest him? Is he not a prophet?"

Several of the multitude followed Jesus into the temple, but the rest remained listening to the priests, who cried more vehemently than ever: "Away with the prophet! He is a false teacher."

But Nathanael, seizing the opportunity, thus addressed the remainder of the multitude: "Oh, thou blinded people, wilt thou run after the innovator, and forsake Moses, the prophets, and thy priests? Fearest thou not that the curse which the law denounces against the apostate will crush thee? Would you cease to be the chosen people?"

The crowd shaken by this appeal, responded sullenly: "That would we not."

Nathanael pressed his advantage. "Who," he asked, "has to watch over the purity of the law? Is it not the holy Sanhedrin of the people of Israel? To whom will you listen; to us or to him? To us or to him who has proclaimed himself the expounder of a new law?"

Then the multitude cried all together: "We hear you! we follow you!" Nathanael continued: "Down with him, then, this man full of deceit and error!"

The people replied: "Yes, we stand side by side with you! Yes, we are Moses' disciples!" and the priests answered, speaking all together: "The God of your fathers will bless you for that."

At this moment loud and angry voices were heard approaching down the narrow street that led to the house of Annas, the high priest. The priests and Pharisees listened eagerly. As they caught the word "revenge" they turned to each other with exultant looks. Meanwhile Dathan, a merchant, the chief of the traders who had been driven from the temple, was seen to be leading on his fellow merchants, who were lifting up their hands and weeping as they recounted their losses. They shouted confusedly as they came: "This insult must be punished! Revenge! Revenge! He shall pay dearly for his insolence. Money, oil, salt; doves—he must pay for all. Where is he, that he may experience our vengeance?"

The priests replied: "He has conveyed himself away."

"Then," cried the traders, "we will pursue him."

But Nathanael, seeing what advantage might result from the discontent of the merchants, arrested their pursuit. "Stay friends," he said; "the faction that follows this man is at present too large. If you attacked them it might cause a dangerous fight, which the Roman sword would finish. Trust to us. He shall not escape punishment."

And the priests who stood around Nathanael cried: "With us and for us: that is your salvation!" Then Dathan and his friends exclaimed triumphantly: "Our victory is near."

Nathanael assured of the control of the multitude, continued: "We are now going to inform the council of the Sanhedrin of today's events."

The traders impatiently exclaimed: "We will go with you. We must have satisfaction."

But Nathanael dissuaded them, saying: "Come in an hour's time to the forecourt of the high priest. I will plead your cause in the council, and bring forward your complaint."

And as Nathanael and the priests and the Pharisees went out, the traders and the people cheered them, crying aloud: "We have Moses! Down with every other! We are for Moses' law to the death! Praise be to our fathers! Praise to our father's God!"

Then the high priests and the rulers and the elders gathered together late in the night in the council of the Sanhedrin. In the highest place sat Caiaphas with his jewelled breast-plate, in robes of white embroidered with gold. A vestment of green and gold covered his shoulders, and on his head he wore a white-horned mitre adorned with golden bells, which added to the majesty of his aspect. Annas, the aged high priest, sat on his left. Nathanael, also on the raised dais, was on the right. Below him sat the rabbis in blue velvet, while seated around were Pharisees, scribes and doctors of the law.

Caiaphas, whose white hair and beard showed that he was well stricken in years, was still in the full vigor of life. As president of the Sanhedrin, he briefly opened the session:

"Honored brothers, fathers and teachers of the people, an extraordinary occurrence is the occasion of the present extraordinary assembly. Listen to it from the mouth of our worthy brother."

Then Nathanael arose, and standing on the right hand of Caiaphas, said: "Is it allowed; O, fathers, to say a word?"

All answered: "Yes, speak! speak!"

Then said Nathanael: "Marvel not, O fathers, that you should be called together at so late an hour for the transaction of business. It must be only too well known to you what we have with shame been compelled to see today with our own eyes. You have seen the triumphal progress of the Galilean through the Holy City. You have heard the Hosannas of the befooled populace. You have perceived how this ambitious man arrogates to himself the office of the high priest. What now lacks for the destruction of all civil and ecclesiastical order? Only a few steps further, and the law of Moses is upset by the innovations of this misleader. The sayings of our forefathers are despised, the fasts and purifications abolished, the Sabbath desecrated, the priests of God deprived of their office, and the holy sacrifices are at an end."

As Nathanael concluded, all the fathers of the council exclaimed with one voice: "True—most true." As he had been speaking they had been interchanging notes of appreciative and sympathetic comment. But it was not until Caiaphas spoke that the Sanhedrin was roused to the highest pitch of excitement. Caiaphas, who spoke with great fire and fervor, thus addressed the rulers of Israel: "And more than all this. Encouraged by the success of his efforts, he will proclaim himself King of Israel (murmurs of alarm and indignation), then the land will be distracted with civil war and revolt, and the Romans will come with their armies and bring destruction upon our land and our people. Woe is me for the children of Israel, for the Holy City, and for the temple of the Lord, if no barrier is opposed to the evil while there is yet time! It is indeed high time. We must be the saviors of Israel. Today must a resolution be passed, and whatever is resolved upon must be carried out without regard to any other consideration. Do we all agree to this?"

And all the Sanhedrin as one man cried out: "We do."

Up sprang a priest to emphasize his vote:

"A stop must be put to the course of this misleader."

Caiaphas then said: "Give your opinion without reserve as to what should be done."

And then a rabbi arose and said: "If I may be permitted to declare my opinion unreservedly, I must assert that we ourselves are to blame that things have come to such a pass. Against this onrushing ruin much too mild measures have been employed. Of what avail have been our disputations with him, or what has it profited that we have by our questionings, put him in a dilemma; that we have pointed, out the errors in his teaching and his violations of the law? Nay, of what use has been even the excommunication pronounced on all who acknowledged him as the Messiah? All this was labor in vain. Men turn their backs on us, and all the world runs after him. To restore peace to Israel, that must be done which ought to have been done long ago—we must arrest him and throw him into prison. That is the only way to put an end to his evil influence."

The suggestion was hailed with enthusiasm, and springing to their feet they cried: "Yea, that must be done!"

Then a third priest stood up and said: "Once he is in prison, the credulous people will no longer be attracted by the fascination of his manner or the charm of his discourse. When they have no more miracles to gape at; he will soon be forgotten."

And a fourth priest exulted as he added: "In the darkness of his dungeon let him make his light shine and proclaim his Messiahship to the walls of the jail."

Then it was the turn of the Pharisees. The first said: "He has been allowed long enough to lead the people astray and to denounce as hypocrisy the strict virtue of the Holy Order of the Pharisees. Let him suffer in fetters for his contempt."

A second Pharisee added complacently: "The enthusiasm of his hangers-on will soon cool down when he who has promised them freedom is himself in chains."

By this time it was evident all the council was of one mind. Then Annas, the venerable high priest, arose and addressed the Sanhedrin with much emotion: "Now, venerable priests, a ray of confidence and joy penetrates to my breast when I see your unanimous resolution. Alas! an unspeakable grief has weighed down my soul at the sight of the onward progress of the false teachings of this Galilean. It seemed as if I had lived to old age but in order to have the misfortune of seeing the downfall of our holy law. But now I will not despair. The God of our fathers still lives, and he is with us. If you have the courage to act boldly, and to stand firmly and faithfully together, there is safety at hand. Take courage, steadfastly pursue the aim in view, and be the deliverer of Israel, and undying fame will be your reward."

With one accord all answered and said: "We are of one mind," while the priests added, shouting eagerly, "Israel must be saved!"

Then Caiaphas began: "All honor to your unanimous resolution, worthy brethren, but now let me have the benefit of your wise counsels how we can most safely bring this deceiver into our power."

"It might be dangerous," remarked the first Pharisee, "to seize him now at the time of the feast. In the streets or in the temple he is everywhere surrounded by a mob of infatuated followers. It could easily lead to an uproar."

Then cried all the priests together with a loud voice, as if impatient that one should speak at a time: "But something must be done at once. The matter brooks no delay. Perhaps at the feast he might raise a commotion, and then it might come to pass that we should be consigned to the place which we have destined for him."

"No delay;" cried some other priests, "no delay!"

Then the second Pharisee stood up and said: "We cannot now seize him openly with the strong hand. We must carry out our scheme cunningly and in secret. Let us find out where he usually spends the night; then we could fall upon him unobserved and take him into custody."

Nathanael sprang to his feet, for the auspicious moment had come,—the furious merchants from the temple were without in the courtyard. "To track the fox to his lair will not be difficult. We could then soon find someone to help, if it should please the high council to offer a large reward."

Caiaphas at once put the resolution to the Sanhedrin. Rising from his seat he said, "If you, assembled fathers, agree, then in the name of the high council I will issue notice that whoever knows of his nightly resort, and will inform us of the same, will be rewarded for his pains."

With one voice the rulers and chief priests and scribes cried out, rising from their seats, "We are all agreed."

Then said Nathanael, "Without doubt we could secure the services, as informers, of those men whom the Galilean today has injured so deeply in the sight of all the people, driving them with a scourge out of the temple. From of old they were zealous of the law, but now they are thirsting for revenge against him who has made so unheard-of an attack upon their privileges."

"But where," said Caiaphas, "are these traders to be found?"

"They are waiting," said Nathanael, "in readiness in the outer court. I have promised them to be the advocate of their cause before the holy Sanhedrin, and they await our decision."

"Worthy priest," said Caiaphas, "inform them that the high council is disposed to listen to their grievance, and bring them in."

Nathanael as he went said, "This will be a joy to them and of great use to us."

When Nathanael left the hall, Caiaphas addressed the council with words of cheer: "The God of our fathers has not withdrawn his hand from us. Moses still watches over us. If only we can succeed in gathering around us a nucleus of men out of the people then I no longer dread the result. Friends and brethren, let us be of good courage, our fathers look down upon us from Abraham's bosom."

"God bless our high priest!" rang through the hall as Nathanael, followed by Dathan and the other traders, returned to his place. He introduced them thus: "High priests and chosen teachers! These men, worthy of our blessing, appear before this assembly in order to lodge a complaint against the notorious Jesus of Nazareth, who has today insulted them in the temple in an unheard-of fashion and brought them to grief."

Then with one voice the traders, led by Dathan, cried out, "We beseech the council to procure us satisfaction. The council ought to support our righteous demands."

The priests and Pharisees responded eagerly, "You shall have satisfaction, we will answer for that."

Then ensued the following dialogue between the traders and the Sanhedrin:

The Traders: "Has not the council authorized us to display openly in the court of the temple all things useful for the sacrifice?"

A Priest: "Yes, that has been sanctioned. Woe be to those who disturb you in the exercise of this right!"

The Traders: "And the Galilean has driven us out with a scourge. And the tables of the money changers has he overturned, and released the doves. We demand satisfaction."

Caiaphas: "That you should have satisfaction the law decrees. Your losses will be made good in the meantime out of the temple treasury" (joy among the traders). "But that the offender himself may be duly punished it is necessary for us to have your help. What can we do so long as he is not in our power?"

The Traders: "He goes daily to the temple; there he can easily be arrested and carried off."

Caiaphas: "That will not do. You know that as he has a multitude of excited followers such a course might lead to a dangerous uproar. The thing must be done quietly."

The Traders: "That could be done best at night-time."

Caiaphas: "If you could find out where he retires at night he would soon be without tumult in our hands. Then would you not only have the delight of seeing him chastised, but also a considerable reward would fall to your lot."

Nathanael: "And you would also have rendered good service to the law of Moses if you assist in this."

Then all the traders cried out together: "You can depend upon us, we will spare no trouble."

And all the priests and Pharisees congratulated themselves that the business was going well. Dathan, conspicuous by his apparel, then volunteered a statement. He said: "I know one of his followers from whom I could easily gain some information if I could offer him a sufficient reward."

Caiaphas at once authorized him, "If thou findest such a one make all necessary promises in our name. Only don't loiter; we must attain our end before the feast."

Annas enjoined the strictest silence, to which with one voice the traders responded, "We swear it," and then Caiaphas proceeded to urge upon them the need of creating a party on their side among the people. "If, my good fellows, you really desire fully to glut your longing for revenge, then take care and use every means to kindle in others the same holy zeal which glows in you."

They answered that they had not waited for his prompting, but had already brought several others over to their side. "We will not rest until the whole populace is roused against him."

Annas and Caiaphas applauded their zeal. "You will thereby merit the greatest gratitude from the council," said Annas, and Caiaphas chimed in, "Openly will ye then be honored before all the people as you have been today put to shame before them by this presumptuous man."

"Our life for the law of Moses and the holy Sanhedrin," then cried the traders. "The God of Abraham guide you," said Caiaphas dismissing them, and they left the hall crying aloud, "Long live Moses! long live the high priests and the Sanhedrin! Even today may the role of the Galilean be played out!"

Then Caiaphas addressed these parting words to the council: "As though refreshed by sweet slumbers, I live once more. With such men as these we can put everything through. Now we shall see who will triumph,—he with his followers to whom he is always preaching love,—a love which is to include publicans and sinners and even the Gentiles also,—or we with this troop inspired by hate and revenge which we are sending against him. There can be no doubt to which side the victory will incline."

"The God of our fathers give us the victory!" said Annas; "joy in my old age will renew my youth!"

Then said Caiaphas, "Let us now break up, looking forward with confidence to the joy of victory. Praised be our fathers!"

And all the assembly with a deep, sonorous voice exclaimed, "Praised be the God of Abraham, of Isaac, and of Jacob!"

CHAPTER II

JESUS' LAST JOURNEY TO JERUSALEM

> People of God behold; thy Savior is nigh to thee!
> He is come who was promised thee long ago.
> Oh! hear him, follow his guidance
> Blessing and life will he bring to thee.
>
> But blind and deaf Jerusalem has shown herself;
> She has thrust back the hands held out to her in love;
> Therefore also the Highest has turned away his face,
> And lets her sink to destruction.

Jesus, accompanied by all his disciples, set out to pay his last visit to Bethany. Peter, with his staff in hand, walked with John beside the master. Judas was present, with disheveled locks and haggard look, James the Greater and James the Less, and Andrew and Thomas, and the rest of the disciples.

Then Jesus spoke unto them and said: "You know, dear disciples, that after two days is the feast of the Passover. So now let us make one last visit to our friends in Bethany, and then go to Jerusalem, where in these days all will be fulfilled which has been written by the prophets concerning the Son of Man."

The disciples understood not his saying, and after some questioning among themselves Philip ventured to address Jesus, saying unto him, "Has the day then really come at last when thou wilt restore the kingdom to Israel?"

Jesus looked upon Philip with tender compassion, and said unto him, "Then shall the Son of Man be delivered up to the Gentiles, and shall be mocked and spat upon and they will crucify him; but on the third day he will rise again."

Then said John in a voice that trembled with emotion, as the other disciples gazed at each other in horror, "Dear master, what dark and terrible words thou speakest. What are we to understand by them? Make it clear unto us."

Then Jesus answered and said unto him, "The hour is now come when the Son of Man shall be glorified. Verily, verily, I say unto you, if a corn of wheat does not fall into the ground and die, it abideth alone, but if it die it bringeth forth much fruit. Now is the judgment of the world. Now shall the prince of this world be cast out. And I, if I be lifted up from the earth, will draw all men unto me."

Then were the breasts of the disciples troubled, for they could not understand what these things meant. Thaddeus said to Simon, "What does he mean by this speech?"

Simon replied with a puzzled air, "Why does he compare himself to a grain of corn?"

Then said Andrew unto him, "Lord, thou speakest at once of shame and of victory. I know not how to reconcile those ideas in my mind."

Jesus said, "That which is now dark to you as the night will be as clear as the day. I have told you before that you may not lose courage whatever may happen. Believe and hope. When the tribulation is passed, then you will see and understand."

Thomas answered and said unto him, "What I cannot understand is that thou shouldst speak of suffering and of death. Have we not heard from the prophets that the Messiah shall live forever? What can thine enemies do unto thee? One single word from thee would annihilate them all."

Jesus said unto him, "Thomas, reverence the secret counsels of God which thou canst not fathom."

Then, turning to the others, he said, "Yet a little while is the light with you. Walk while you have the light, lest darkness overtake you."

By this time they had approached near the village of Bethany, and there met them one Simon, after whom there came Lazarus, who was raised from the dead, with Martha, his sister, and Mary Magdalene, the latter tall, dark, with long black hair, in dark blue dress with a yellow mantle.

Simon pressed forward; he was an old man and he hastened to meet Jesus. "Welcome, best of teachers, O what joy that thou shouldst honor my house with thy entrance. Dear friends, be also welcome," he exclaimed; but he was startled to hear the reply, "Simon, for the last time I, with my disciples, lay claim to thy hospitality."

Simon replied in grief, "Say not so, Lord. Often still shall Bethany afford thee brief repose."

By this time Lazarus drew near; he was of less than middle stature and silent, as if his sojourn in the other world left him little to speak of in this. "See," said Jesus, "there is our friend Lazarus."

"My Lord," cried Lazarus, embracing him, "the vanquisher of death, lifegiver and Lord, I see thee once again and hear the voice that called me from the grave."

Then hastened the Magdalene to his side, and kneeling down, "Rabbi," she exclaimed; Martha also said, "Welcome, Rabbi."

Then Jesus blessed them, saying, "God's blessing be upon you!"

Then Martha asked, "Wilt thou Lord, grant me the happiness of serving thee?" while the Magdalene timidly inquired, "Wilt thou despise a token of love and gratitude from me?"

And Jesus replied with tenderness, "Do, good souls, that which you purpose to do."

Then said Simon, "Best of masters, come under my roof and refresh thyself and thy disciples."

So Jesus entered into Simon's house, exclaiming, "Peace be upon this house," to which the disciples added, speaking together, "And to all that dwell therein." Then said Simon, "Lord, all is ready, set thee down at table and bid thy disciples sit down also."

Then Jesus sat down to meat, saying, "Let us now, beloved disciples, enjoy with thanks the gifts which our Father in heaven bestows upon us through Simon, his servant. O Jerusalem, would that my coming were as dear to thee as it is to these, my friends! But thou are stricken with blindness."

"Yes, Lord," remarked Lazarus; "O best of masters, dangers threaten thee. The Pharisees are anxiously wondering whether thou wilt come up to the Passover. They are eagerly watching for thy destruction."

Simon said, "Stay here, Lord; here thou art safe."

Then Peter interposed with an entreaty, "Lord, it is good to be here. Remain here, in the seclusion of this house, served by faithful love, till the gathering storm be passed."

But Jesus rebuked him sternly, saying: "Get thee behind me, tempter. Thou savorest not of the things that are of God, but those that be of men. Can the reaper tarry in the shade while the ripe harvest awaits him? The Son of Man came not to be ministered unto, but to minister and to give his life a ransom for many."

Then the dark-browed Judas spoke, uttering this time the thought of all. "But, master, what will become of us if thou givest up thy life?"

A chorus of approval burst from all the disciples, "Ah, all our hopes would then be destroyed."

"Trouble not yourselves," said Jesus, "I have power to lay down my life and I have power to take it up again. This commandment have I received of my Father."

And lo, while they were yet speaking, Mary Magdalene silently approached Jesus, carrying in her hand a bottle of ointment of spikenard, very precious, which she poured over his head as she murmured but one word, "Rabbi." And Jesus also said but one word, "Mary," but his tone was full of tenderness and love.

As the perfume of the ointment filled the room the disciples spoke among themselves. "What an exquisite odor!" said Thomas, leaning past the others to look.

"It is real oil of spikenard, very costly," said Bartholomew.

Thaddeus added, "Such an honor has never been shown to our master."

But Judas could not contain himself. He growled from his distant seat, "To what purpose is this waste? The money might have been much better expended."

"Yes," said Thomas, "I almost think so, too."

Then Magdalene, heedless of the murmurs of the disciples, knelt down and anointed Jesus' feet and wiped them with her long black tresses. Jesus, after a little while, noticing the muttering down the table, asked, "What are you saying to each other? Why do you condemn that which is done only from grateful love."

The Magdalene knelt back, sheltering herself as it were behind her Lord.

Judas blurted out impetuously his dissatisfaction. "To pour out so much costly ointment, what wasteful extravagance!"

"Friend Judas," said Jesus, "look at me. Is what is done for me, thy master, waste?"

Judas said, "I know that thou lovest not useless expense; the ointment might have been sold and the poor helped with the money!" Hearing Judas' answer he half turned away and looked wearily upward, folding his hands.

"Judas," said Jesus somewhat sternly, "hand upon thy heart now. Is it only pity for the poor which moves thee so much?"

Judas replied, "At least three hundred pence could have been got for it. What a loss both for the poor and for us."

Then Jesus answered and said, "The poor you have always with you, but me ye have not always." Then he said, "Let her alone, she has wrought a good work on me, for in that she has poured out the ointment upon me, she has anointed me for my burial. Verily I say unto you, wheresoever the gospel will be preached through the whole world, there shall also this which she hath done be told for a memorial of her."

He then said to the disciples, "Let us arise"—and then turning to Simon, his host, he said, "I thank thee, benevolent man, for thy hospitality, the Father will repay it unto thee."

"Say nothing of thanks, master," said Simon; "I know what I owe to thee."

Then Jesus arose and said, "It is time to go hence. Farewell all ye dwellers in this hospitable house. My disciples, follow me."

Peter said unto him, "Lord, wherever thou wilt, only not to Jerusalem."

Jesus answered, "I go where my Father calls me. If it please thee to remain here, Peter, do so." Then Peter declared, "Lord, where thou abidest there will I also abide; whither thou goest there go I also."

Jesus said, "Come then."

The disciples arose and clasping their staffs were ready to depart. Then Jesus turned to Mary Magdalene and Martha and said, "Remain here, beloved! Once more, fare ye well. Dear, peaceful Bethany, never more shall I tarry in thy quiet vale."

Simon, sore troubled in speech as he heard these words, said unto him, "Then wilt thou really depart hence forever?"

Mary Magdalene threw herself at his feet and said, "Alas, I am filled with terrible forebodings. Friend of my soul! My heart—oh! my heart—it will not let thee go!"

Jesus said unto her, "Stand up, Mary. The night cometh and the winter storms come blustering on. But be comforted. In the early morning in the garden of spring, thou wilt see me again."

Lazarus exclaimed, "Oh! my friend, my benefactor!"

"Alas!" cried Martha, "thou art going; and comest thou back nevermore?"

Jesus said, "The Father wills it, beloved. Wherever I am I bear you ever with me in my heart, and wherever you are, my blessings will follow you. Farewell."

And behold as they turned to go, there met them Mary, the mother of Jesus, with her companions. Mary had a white mantle round her head, from beneath which her long dark hair hung down. She hastened to her son, crying, "Jesus, dearest son, I hastened after thee with my friends, in eager longing to see thee once more before thou goest, all whither?"

Jesus clasped her hands gently and replied, "Mother, I am on the way to Jerusalem."

"To Jerusalem," said his mother. "There is the temple of Jehovah, whither I once carried thee in my arms to offer thee to the Lord."

"Mother," said Jesus in solemn sadness, "the hour is come when according to the will of the Father I shall offer myself. I am ready to complete the sacrifice which the Father demands from me."

"Ah," cried Mary with bitter and piteous cry, "I foresee what kind of a sacrifice that will be."

John and Mary Magdalene had joined the mother of Jesus, and the two Marys standing together united their lament.

"How much we had wished," said the Magdalene, "to keep back the master and make him remain with us."

"It is of no use," said Simon gloomily, "his purpose is fixed."

Then said Jesus to his mother, tenderly beholding her, "My hour is come."

All the disciples cried, "Oh, ask the Father that he should let it pass by."

Then all the women said, "The Father has always listened to thee."

But Jesus said: "How is my soul troubled, and what shall I say? Father, deliver me from this hour! But for this hour came I into the world."

But Mary hearing him, exclaimed as in a trance, "Oh, venerable Simon, now will be fulfilled that which thou once prophesied to me, 'A sword shall pierce through thine own soul!'" And as she spoke Mary Magdalene gently supported her from falling.

Jesus said in terms of gentle reproach, "Mother, the will of the Father was also ever sacred to thee." His word rallied her courage and she replied, "It is so to me still. I am the handmaid of the Lord. What he requires of me I will bear patiently. But one thing I beg of thee, my son."

"What desirest thou, my mother?"

"That I may go with thee into the fierce conflict of suffering, yea, even unto death!"

"Oh, what love!" exclaimed John, who stood tearfully beside the two Marys, wistfully looking for some ray of hope to illumine the darkness beyond.

Jesus embraced her lovingly. "Dear mother, thou wilt suffer with me, thou wilt fight with me in my death struggle, but thou wilt also rejoice with me in my victory, therefore be comforted."

"Oh, God!" she cried in heartrending accents, "give me strength that my heart may not break."

"We all weep with thee, thou best of mothers," said the holy women, adding their tears to those of the mother of Jesus.

"I will go with thee, my son, to Jerusalem," said Mary.

And the holy women declared they also would go with her.

But Jesus, holding her hand, tenderly forbade her: "Later you may go thither, but not now. For the present stay with our friends at Bethany. I commend to you, O faithful souls, my beloved mother, with those who have followed her here."

Eagerly the Magdalene accepted the charge.

"After thee," she exclaimed, "there is no one dearer to us than thy mother."

But even at the eleventh hour Lazarus interposed one last word of entreaty: "If only thou, O master, couldst remain!"

Not noticing this, Jesus said, "Comfort ye one another. After two days you may come up together to Jerusalem, to be there on the great day of the feast."

Mary said: "As thou wilt, my son."

But the holy women said: "How sadly will the hours pass when thou art far from us."

Then Jesus spoke to his mother and said, "Mother, mother, for the tender love and motherly care which thou hast shown to me for the three and thirty years of my life, receive the warmest thanks of thy son." And stooping down he kissed her. Then raising his head, he said, "The Father calls me. Fare thee well, best of mothers."

Mary asked him: "My son, where shall I see thee again?"

And Jesus replied: "There, beloved mother, where the Scripture shall be fulfilled: 'He was led as a lamb to the slaughter, and he opened not his mouth.'"

Mary sobbing, cried aloud, "Jesus, thy mother, oh! Oh, God, my son!"

Half fainting she was held up by the holy women, who exclaimed, "O beloved, faithful mother!"

The disciples departed, muttering, "We cannot endure it. What will be the end of all this?"

Then burst from their lips the despairing cry, "Alas, what affliction lies before us all?"

But Jesus said, "Sink not in the first conflict. Hold fast by me."

And the disciples repeated, "Yea, master, fast by thee."

Lazarus and the women looking back after Christ as he passed out of sight, exclaimed, "Ah! our dear teacher," while Simon said, "He brought happiness to my house."

Simon then turned tenderly to Mary and said: "Come, mother, and condescend to enter in." "One consolation remains to us in tribulation," said Mary Magdalene, and Martha added, "To have the mother of our Lord with us." Turning to the other women, Lazarus said, "And you, beloved ones, come with us, we will share our woe and tears together."

All then together went into the house, Mary Magdalene supporting the mother of Jesus.

Now as they came unto Jerusalem they looked down upon the whole city which lay before them. Then said John unto Jesus, "Master, behold what a splendid view of Jerusalem from this spot!"

Matthew said, "The majestic temple, how splendidly it is built."

Jesus was troubled in spirit, and after gazing for a moment over the city, clasped his hands in grief and cried, "O Jerusalem, Jerusalem, O that thou hadst known even in this thy day the things that belong unto thy peace! but now they are hidden from thine eyes!"

Jesus wept.

His disciples beholding him weep were amazed. At last Peter ventured to say, "Master, why grievest thou so sorely?"

Jesus answered, "My Peter, the fate of this unhappy city goes to my heart."

Then said John, "Lord, tell us what shall this fate be?"

Jesus answered and said unto them, "The days will come when her enemies will make a trench about her walls and close her in on every side, and lay her even with the ground. She and her children within her walls will be dashed to the earth, and not one stone will be left upon another."

Andrew, giving expression to the general consternation, asked, "Wherefore shall the city have so sad a doom?"

Jesus said, "Because she hath not known the day of her visitation. Alas! she who hath slain the prophets will kill the Messiah himself."

Then spoke all the disciples together, "What a terrible deed!"

James, the elder, said, "God forbid that the city of Jehovah should bring such a curse upon herself."

And John with pleading voice added, "Dearest master, for the sake of the holy city and the temple, I beg of thee go not thither, so that the opportunity may be wanting to those evil men to do the worst."

"Or," said Peter, "go thither and display thyself in all thy majesty, so that the good may rejoice and the evil tremble."

"Yes," cried all the twelve eagerly, "do that."

Philip said, "Strike down thine enemies!" and all added earnestly, "And set up the kingdom of God among men!"

Jesus answered, "Children, that which you desire shall come to pass in due time, but my ways are appointed to me by my father, and thus saith the Lord, 'My thoughts are not as your thoughts, and my ways are not as your ways.'"

Then, as if to cut short a useless discussion, he said, "Peter!" Peter replied, "What wilt thou, Lord?" and the Lord continued, "It is now the first day of unleavened bread, in which the law commands that we should eat the Passover; you, both Peter and John, go forward and prepare the Passover that we may eat it in the evening."

Peter and John, who stood the one on the left and the other on the right, asked, "Where wilt thou, Lord, that we prepare the Passover?"

Jesus said, "When you come into the city there shall meet you a man bearing a pitcher of water, follow ye him and wheresoever he shall go in, say ye to the good man of the house, 'The master says, Where is the guest-chamber that I may eat the Passover with my disciples?' and he will show you a large upper chamber furnished and prepared; there make ready the Passover."

"Thy blessing, O best of masters!" said Peter. He and John knelt on either side of their Lord, Jesus placed his right hand on the head of John and his left hand on the head of Peter, exclaiming, "God's blessing be with you!"

Peter and John having departed, Jesus said to the others, "Accompany me for the last time to the house of my Father."

Then Judas, who had for some time past stood apart, came forward and said, "But, master, allow me; if thou wilt really leave us, make some arrangement for our future support. Look here," he added, pointing to the small bag almost empty of coin, which he carried in his girdle, "there is not enough here for one day more."

Jesus looked upon him and said, "Judas, do not be more anxious than is needful."

But Judas went on muttering and looking not at his Lord, but at the bag, "How well the value of that uselessly wasted ointment would have lain therein! how long we could have lived on it without care!"

Jesus reproved him, saying, "You have never lacked anything hitherto and, believe me, that what is necessary will not fail you in time to come."

Judas said, "But, master, when thou art no longer with us our good friends will soon draw back, and then we shall be left in sore distress."

Jesus said unto him, "Friend Judas, beware lest thou fall into temptation."

The other disciples who had listened to this conversation then interrupted, saying altogether, "Judas, trouble not the master so much."

Judas retorted, "Who will take thought if I do not? Have I not been appointed by the master to carry the bag?"

"Thou hast," said Jesus, "but I fear——"

"And I also fear," interrupted Judas, "that soon it will be empty and remain so."

Then Jesus went close up to him and said gravely and gently, "Judas, forget not thy warning. Arise, now let us go hence, I desire to be in the house of my Father."

Jesus then, followed by his disciples, excepting Judas, passed on to the city.

Judas, being left alone, said to himself, "Shall I follow him any longer. I do not much care to do so. The master's conduct to me is very inexplicable. His great deeds allowed us to hope that he would restore again the kingdom to Israel. But he does not seize the opportunities that offer themselves, and now he constantly talks of parting and dying, and puts us off with mysterious words about a future which lies too far off in the dim distance for me. I am tired of hoping and waiting. I can see very well, that with him there is no prospect of anything but continued poverty and humiliation,—and instead of the sharing, as we expected, in his glorious kingdom, we shall perhaps be persecuted and thrown into prison with him. I will draw back. It was a good thing that I was always prudent and cautious, and have now and then laid aside a trifle out of the bag in case of need. How useful I should find those 300 pence now which the foolish woman threw away on a useless mark of respect. If, as seems likely, the society is about to dissolve, they would have remained in my hands—then I should have been safe for a long while to come. As it is, I must consider the question, where and how I can find subsistence."

As he stood alone under the trees, perplexed and troubled, Dathan appeared in the distance, and, spying Judas, said to himself, "The occasion is favorable. He is alone and seems much perplexed. I must try everything in order to secure him."

Then stepping forward he laid his hand upon the shoulder of Judas, exclaiming, "Friend Judas!"

Judas started as if a serpent had stung him and striking his head with his hand cried, "Who calls?"

"A friend," said Dathan; "has anything sad happened to thee? Thou art so absorbed in thought?"

Judas, staring wildly, asked, "Who art thou?"

"Thy friend, thy brother," cried Dathan.

Judas, staring backward, exclaimed: "Thou art my friend, my brother?"

"At least," said Dathan, "I wish to be so. How is it with the master? I also would like to become one of his disciples."

Judas said, "One of his disciples?"

"Why?" said Dathan, "hast thou then forsaken him? Are things not well with him? Tell me that I may know how to act."

Then Judas said unto him, "Canst thou keep silence?"

"Be assured of that," said Dathan.

"Then," answered Judas, "it is no longer going well with him. He says himself his last hour has come." And then Judas rapidly ran over the various predictions of disaster which he had heard from the lips of Jesus. "I intend to forsake him, for he will yet bring us all to ruin. See here," said he, producing the almost empty purse, "I am treasurer, see how it stands with us."

"Friend," said Dathan, shrugging his shoulders, "I shall remain as I am." At this moment six of Dathan's companions came up.

Judas, alarmed, asked, "Who are these? I will not say another word."

"Stay, friend," said one of the newcomers, "you will not regret it."

"Why have you come here?" asked Judas.

"We were going back to Jerusalem and we will bear thee company if it please thee."

Judas, suspiciously eyeing them, asked, "Do you also perhaps wish to go after the master?"

Then said the traders, "Has he gone to Jerusalem?"

"For the last time," said Judas, "so he says."

"What!" said they, "for the last time? Is he then never going to leave the land of Judea again?"

"Why do you ask me this so eagerly?" said Judas, "do you wish to become his followers?"

"Why not?" said the traders with a laugh, "if the prospects are good;" and Dathan added, "Explain to us, Judas, the meaning of thy words that he would bring you all to ruin."

And Judas replied: "He tells us always to take no thought for the morrow, but if today anything happened we should all be as poor as beggars. Does a master care thus for his own?"

"Truly," said the traders, "the lookout is bad."

Then Judas related once more the story of Mary Magdalene's waste of precious ointment. "And at the same time this very day he permitted the most senseless waste which a foolish woman was guilty of, thinking to obtain honor; and when I found fault with this I only met with reproachful words and looks."

"And thou canst still care for him after that?" said the traders contemptuously, "and art still willing to remain with him? Thou shouldst take thought for thine own future; it is high time."

"So I have been thinking," said Judas, "but how can I find a good opening?"

Then said Dathan, "Thou hast not long to seek, for the fairest opportunity is awaiting thee."

"Where? How?" said Judas eagerly.

"Hast thou not heard," said the traders, "of the proclamation of the council? Such a good opportunity of making thy fortune thou wilt never find again thy whole life long."

Judas' eyes gleamed. "What proclamation?" he asked.

The traders said, "Whosoever gives information as to the nightly resort of Jesus of Nazareth shall receive a large reward."

"A large reward!" said Judas.

"Now who," said they, "can earn it easier than thou?"

Dathan muttered to himself, "We have nearly attained our end."

The traders pressed Judas anew, "Brother, don't neglect this good fortune."

Judas said hesitatingly, "A fair opportunity. Shall I let it slip?"

Then struck in Dathan, "The reward is not all. The council will look after thee in the future. Who knows what might not yet come of it for thee!"

"Consent, friend! Strike the bargain," cried all the traders together.

Judas hesitated one moment and then clasped Dathan's hand, saying, "Well, be it so."

"Come, Judas," said Dathan, "we will bring thee straightway to the council." But Judas said, "No, I must first go after the master, and so obtain information in order to make things sure."

Dathan said, "Well, then, we will go to the council and report you in the meantime. But when and where shall we meet?"

"In three hours you will find me in the street of the temple," replied Judas.

Judas then shook hands all around with the traders. "Done!" exclaimed Judas, as Dathan and the traders left him.

Judas was now alone. He walked to and fro under the trees and said to himself: "My word is given; I shall not repent of it. Shall I avoid the good fortune which is coming to meet me? Yes, my fortune is made. I will do what I promised, but will make them pay me in advance. If then the priests succeed in taking him prisoner, if his reign is over—I have assured my own prospects and will besides become famous throughout all Judea, as a man who has helped to save the law of Moses, and shall reap praise and glory. But if the master should gain the victory, then—yes, then I will cast me down repentant at his feet, for he is good. I have never seen him drive the penitent from him. He will take me back again and then I shall have the credit of bringing about the decision. Anyhow, I'll take good care to leave a bridge behind so that should I be unable to go forward I can return. The plan is well thought out. Judas, thou art a prudent man. And yet I feel a little afraid to meet the master, for I shall not be able to bear his keen, searching look, and my comrades will see by my face that I am a——No, I will not be that. I am no traitor! What am I going to do but let the Jews know where the master is to be found? That is no betrayal. Betrayal is something more than that. Away with these fancies! Courage, Judas, thy future is at stake."

Judas, who had started with horror when he first mentioned the word traitor, resolved to play his appointed role and departed to find Jesus.

CHAPTER III

THE LAST SUPPER

>O Judas, art thou blinded quite
>By untamed greed of gold and gear?
>And would thou sell thy master dear
>For base gain? Shudders not thy soul in dire affright?
>Thy lot has passed into the night,
>Already doth thy doom appear.
>
>"'Tis one of you that shall betray,"
>Three times the Lord thus spoke to him—
>Who's purposed his own soul to slay—
>Yet is his conscience dull and dim,
>For Satan rules his heart within
>And lust for gold that's won by sin.
>
>"Oh Judas! but one moment stay.
>Oh! finish not this foulest deed!"
>But no! for deaf and blind with greed,
>To the council Judas hastes away,
>And there repeats in evil trade,
>The bargain once with Dathan made.

And it came to pass that when Peter and John were still on their way to Jerusalem, Baruch, the servant of Mark, came out into the street with a pitcher of water, which he went to get filled at the well.

As he went he said to himself, "There is a great deal of business today, there will be no lack of work this Passover; from the great crowd of pilgrims we can expect nothing else. My master must expect many guests as he is already making so much to-do in the house." When he was drawing the water John and Peter came upon him.

"See," said they, "there is someone at the well."

Baruch, not noticing them, went on drawing the water, saying,

"There must be something exceptional at this Passover, seeing the way in which the rulers of the council hasten about hither and thither."

As he lifted the pitcher and turned to go Peter said, "This is he who carries the pitcher of water that our master gave us for a sign."

Then said John, "Let us follow him."

Baruch looked around as he came to the door of his master's house, and, seeing the disciples, said, "Will you come in with me, friends? You are welcome."

"We wish," said John, "to speak with your master."

"Perhaps," said Baruch, "you desire to take the Passover with us?"

"Yes," said Peter, "the master desired us to bring this request to your master."

Then said Baruch, "Come with me. It will be a joy to my master to take you into his house. There, see," he said as Mark came out of his house, "there he is himself. See, master, I bring guests."

"Welcome, strangers," said Mark, "how can I serve you?"

Then said Peter unto him, "Our teacher sent us to say unto thee, 'My time is at hand. Where is the hall where I can eat the Passover with my disciples, for my time is at hand. I will keep the Passover in thy house with my disciples.'"

"Oh, joy!" exclaimed Mark, "now I recognize you as the disciples of the miracle-worker who restored to me the light of my eyes. How have I deserved that he should choose my house before all others that are in Jerusalem in which to celebrate the Passover? Oh, fortunate man that I am, that it should be my house which he honors with his presence. Come, dear friends, I will at once show you the hall."

Peter and John replied, "Good friend, we follow thee." And they went into the house and found all things as Jesus had said unto them.

In the upper chamber which Mark had prepared for the Passover Jesus and his disciples stood around a long table. Jesus stood in the center with Peter on his right hand and John on his left. Judas, sullen and scowling, sat next to Peter, and the other disciples were arranged in their order. The table was covered with a white cloth with embroidered edges. On the cloth stood a flagon of wine and several cups, and a plate on which lay a loaf of bread. Jesus, standing in the midst, said unto them, "With longing have I desired to eat this Passover with you before I suffer, for I say unto you I will not any more eat thereof until it be fulfilled in the kingdom of God." Jesus then took the cup, and lifting it with both hands, looked up to heaven and said, "I thank thee for this fruit of the vine." Then drinking of it he passed the cup to Peter, who also drank and passed it to Judas, who in his turn, after drinking, passed it to the next disciple, and so on until it went all around. "Take this," said Jesus, as he passed the cup to Peter, "and divide it amongst yourselves, for I say unto you, I will not drink henceforth of the fruit of the vine until the kingdom of God comes."

Then exclaimed all the disciples together, "Alas, Lord, is this then the last Passover?"

Jesus said unto them, "There is a cup which I will drink with you in the kingdom of God my Father. As it is written, 'Thou shalt make them drink of the river of thy pleasures.'"

Then said Peter unto him, "Master, when this kingdom shall appear, how will the offices be portioned out?"

"Who amongst us," said James the elder, "will have the first place?"

Then Thomas said, "Will each one of us have lordship over a separate land?"

"That would be the best," said Bartholomew; "then no dispute would arise amongst us."

Then Jesus looked upon them and said, "So long a time have I been amongst you and you are still entangled in earthly things? Verily, I appoint unto you, which have continued with me in my temptations, the kingdom which my Father has appointed unto me, that you may eat and drink with me in my kingdom, and sit on thrones judging the twelve tribes of Israel. But, remember, the kings of the Gentiles exercise lordship over them, and they that exercise authority over them are called benefactors, but ye shall not be so. He that is greatest among you, let him be as the least, and the chief as your servant. For whether is greatest he that sitteth at meat or he that serveth? Is not he that sitteth at meat; but I am among you as one that serveth."

Thereupon John removed the long purple robe from the shoulders of Jesus, and handed him a white linen towel, with which he girded himself round the middle. Then came Baruch in, carrying a ewer of water and a basin. As they looked in amazement one at another, Jesus said unto them, "Now sit down, beloved disciples."

Then said the disciples one to another, "What is he going to do?"

Jesus, turning to Peter, said, "Peter, reach me thy foot."

Peter, starting backward in amazement, said, "Lord, dost thou wash my feet?"

Then said Jesus, "What I do thou knowest not now, but thou shalt know hereafter."

Peter replied stoutly, "Lord, thou shalt never to all eternity wash my feet!"

But Jesus said, "If I wash thee not thou shalt have no part with me."

Peter said, "Lord, if it be so, then not my feet only, but also my hands and my head."

But Jesus answered, "He that is washed needeth not save to wash his feet, but is clean every whit." Then stooping down Baruch poured the water over the feet of Peter, and Jesus dried them with a towel. The other disciples took the sandals off their feet, whispering to themselves in wonder as to what this meant. Jesus washed the feet of Judas as those of the others. Last of all he washed the feet of John also. Then he washed his hands, Baruch pouring the water over them. After which he took off the towel, and John placed his mantle once more upon his shoulders. Looking round upon the twelve, he said, "Ye are now clean, but not all." Jesus then seated himself in the midst of them.

Then said Jesus unto them, "Do you know what I have done unto you? Ye call me master and Lord, and ye do well, for so I am. If I then, your Lord and master, have washed your feet, ye also ought to wash one another's feet. For I have given you an example that ye should do as I have done unto you. Verily, verily, the servant is not greater than he that sent him. If ye know these things, happy are ye if ye do them." Then Jesus stood up again and said, "Children, but for a little while shall I be with you. That my memory may never perish from among you, I will leave behind an everlasting memorial, and so I shall ever dwell with you and amongst you. The old covenant which my Father made with Abraham, Isaac and Jacob has reached its end and I say unto you, a new covenant begins, which I solemnly consecrate today with my blood, as the Father has commanded me, and this covenant will last until all be fulfilled." Jesus then took the bread, lifted it up before him, and replacing it on the table, looked up to heaven and blessed it. Then, lifting it up again, he broke it in two, saying, "Take, eat, this is my body which was broken for you." Then passing around the table, he placed a morsel of bread with his own hand in the mouth of each of his disciples. All took it reverently, but Judas bit at it almost as a dog snatcheth meat from its master's hands. After Jesus had returned to his place, he said, "This do in remembrance of me." In like manner he took the cup and blest it and said, "Take this, and drink ye all of it; for this is the cup of the New Testament in my blood, which is shed for you and for many for the remission of sins." Then passing round the table again he gave each of them to drink, and returning to his place he said, "As often as ye do this, do it in remembrance of me." During the time Jesus went round the table administering the bread and wine to his disciples, there was heard in the distance a chorus of angels singing:

> Oh! the lowly love and tender!
> See the Saviour kneeling still
> At the feet of his disciples
> Loving service to fulfil.
> Oh! this love remember ever!
> Love as he has loved, and so
> Unto others render service
> As your Lord has done to you.

Then John in an ecstacy of affection exclaimed, "Oh, best of masters, never will I forget thy love! Thou knowest that I love thee," and leaning forward he laid his head on the breast of Jesus.

The rest of the twelve, who were sitting with clasped hands with the exception of Judas, who sat apart moody and sullen, exclaimed together, "O, Master, who art so full of love for us, ever will we remain united with thee."

Then said Peter, "This holy meal of the new covenant shall ever be celebrated amongst us according to thy commandment."

And Matthew added, "And as often as we shall keep it, we will remember thee!"

Then cried they all, "O, best teacher, O divine one! O best friend and teacher!"

And Jesus looking upon them said, "My children, abide in me, and I in you! As the Father has loved me, so have I also loved you, continue ye in my love. But, alas, must I say it! the hand of him who betrays me is with me at the table!" Judas started, but the confusion of the disciples caused his guilty look to be unnoticed.

Several of the disciples exclaimed, "What! a traitor amongst us!"

"Is it possible?" said Peter.

Then Jesus said, "Verily, verily, I say unto you, one of you shall betray me."

"Lord," said Andrew, "one of us twelve?"

"Yes," replied Jesus, "one of the twelve who dipped his hand in the dish with me shall betray me. So the Scriptures shall be fulfilled. He that eateth bread with me hath lifted up his heel against me."

Thomas and Simon, speaking together with the same thought and same words, asked, "Who can this faithless one be?" while Matthew said, "Lord, thou seest all hearts, thou knowest that it is not I"—and the two James cried, "Name him publicly, the traitor!" Then while these words were on their lips, Judas, fearing lest his silence should be observed, started forward and asked furtively, "Lord, is it I?" but excepting by Jesus his words passed unnoticed.

Thaddeus exclaimed, "I would rather give my life for thee than that such a deed should be done;" and Bartholomew, "I would rather sink into the earth with shame."

Jesus, looking toward Judas said, "Thou hast said it." Turning to the rest, Jesus continued, "The son of man goeth indeed as it is written of him, but woe unto that man by whom the son of man is betrayed; better were it for him that he had never been born!"

Peter, leaning over to John, whispered to him to ask Jesus who it was. Then John whispered to Jesus, saying, "Lord, who is it?"

Jesus answered, speaking so low as to be heard by John alone, "He it is to whom I shall give a sop after having dipped it."

The other apostles who had not heard this kept on asking, "Who can it be?"

Jesus, taking a piece of bread, dipped it into a cup, and placed it in the mouth of Judas, saying, "What thou doest, do quickly."

Then Judas arose and hurried from the room. The disciples seeing his departure wondered among themselves, and Thomas said to Simon, "Why does Judas go away?"

Simon replied, "Probably the master has sent him to buy something," while Thaddeus added, "Or to distribute alms to the poor."

Judas being now gone, Jesus spoke to the eleven, saying, "If God be glorified in him, God shall also glorify him in himself and shall straightway glorify him. Little children, yet a little while I am with you. Ye shall seek me; but as I have said to the Jews, whither I go you cannot come, even so now I say unto you."

Then said Peter unto him, "Lord, whither goest thou?"

Jesus answered, "Whither I go thou canst not follow me now, but thou shalt follow me later."

Peter passionately cried, "Why can I not follow thee now? I will lay down my life for thy sake."

Then Jesus looked upon him with compassion and said, "Wilt thou lay down thy life for my sake? Simon! Simon! Satan hath desired to have thee that he may sift thee as wheat, but I have prayed for thee that thy faith fail not; and when thou art converted, strength thy brethren! This night all ye shall be offended because of me, for it is written, 'I shall smite the shepherd and the sheep of his flock shall be scattered abroad.'"

Peter answered, "Although all shall be offended, yet will not I. Lord, I am ready to go with thee to prison and to death."

Jesus said unto him, "Verily, verily, I say unto thee, Peter, today, even this night, before the cock crow twice, thou shalt deny me thrice."

Then said Peter, rising and clasping his hands, "Even if I should die with thee, I would never deny thee," and the other ten disciples said altogether with a loud voice, "Master, we also will always remain faithful to thee; none of us will ever deny thee."

Then said Jesus unto them, "When I sent you out without purse or scrip, or shoes, lacked ye anything?"

All replied with one voice, "No, nothing."

Then Jesus said, "But now I say unto you, let everyone take his purse and likewise his scrip, and whosoever hath not a sword, let him sell his coat and buy one, for now begins a time of trial; and I say unto you that thus it is written, and it must yet be accomplished in me, 'And he was reckoned among the transgressors!'"

Peter then and Philip each drew a sword from the scabbard which hung at his side under his cloak, exclaiming, "Lord, see here are two swords."

Then said Jesus, "It is enough. Let us stand up and give thanks." Then standing, Jesus and all the disciples said together with a loud voice, "Praise the Lord, all ye people! Praise him, all ye nations! for his merciful kindness is everlasting; the truth of the Lord endureth forever."

Then Jesus, leaving the table, advanced to the foreground and stood for some time with his eyes raised to heaven, the disciples standing on either side watching him with troubled faces. Shortly after he said unto them, "Children, why are ye so sad and why look ye on me so sorrowfully? Let not your heart be troubled; ye believe in God, believe also in me. In my father's house are many mansions. I go to prepare a place for you; and I will come again and receive you unto myself, that where I am there ye may be also. I leave you not as orphans. Peace I leave with you, my peace I give unto you. Keep my commandment. This is my commandment, that ye love one another as I have loved you! By this shall all men know that ye are my disciples, if ye love one another. Hereafter I will not talk much to you, for the prince of this world cometh, although he hath nothing in me. But that the world may know that I love the Father, and as the Father gave me commandment, so do I. Let us go hence."

The Sanhedrin was again in session. Caiaphas presided, Annas as before sat on his left hand and Nathanael on his right. No sooner had all the members of the assembly taken their seats than Caiaphas rose and with radiant countenance began, "Assembled fathers, I have a joyful piece of news to impart to you. The supposed prophet from Galilee will soon, we hope, be in our hands. Dathan, the zealous Israelite, has won over one of the most trusted companions of the Galilean, who will let himself be employed as a guide, so that we may surprise him by night. Both are here, only waiting a summons to appear before us."

"Bring them in," cried with eager voices the priests and Pharisees.

Josue volunteered, "I will call them."

"Yes, call them," said Caiaphas. When Josue left the room Caiaphas asked their counsel as to the price which should be given for the betrayal of Jesus.

Nathanael stood up and said, "The law of Moses gives direction for such a case; a slave is valued at thirty pieces of silver."

The priests laughed thereat and said, "Yea, yea, it is just the price of a slave that the false Messiah is worth."

Then came in Dathan and Judas, Josue conducting them into the presence of the Sanhedrin. Dathan stood forward and said, "Most learned council, I here fulfil the task entrusted to me, and present to the fathers a man who is determined for a suitable reward to deliver our and your enemy into our power. He is a trusted friend of the notorious Galilean and knows his ways and his secret abiding places."

Then said Caiaphas to Judas, "Knowest thou the man whom the council seeks?"

Judas answered, "I have now been a long time in his company and know where he is accustomed to abide."

Then said Caiaphas, "What is thy name?"

He replied, "My name is Judas, and I am one of the twelve."

"Yes, yes," cried several of the priests, "we saw thee often with him."

Caiaphas asked him, "Art thou steadfastly resolved to do our will?"

Judas answered firmly, "I give you my word."

"But," continued Caiaphas, "wilt thou not repent of it? What induced thee to take this step?"

Judas answered, "The friendship between him and me has been cooling down for some time, and now I have quite broken with him."

"What has led to this?" asked Caiaphas.

Judas replied, "There is nothing more to be got from him and indeed I am resolved to remain loyal to lawful authority, that is always the best. What will you give me if I deliver him up to you?"

Then Caiaphas, speaking as if they were promising great things, said, "Thirty pieces of silver, which shall be at once paid over to thee!"

"Hear that, Judas?" cried Dathan, "thirty pieces of silver, what a gain!"

Before Judas could reply, Nathanael sprang to his feet, saying, "And mark thee well, Judas, this is not all! If thou executest this work right well thou shalt be cared for still further."

"And thou mayest become a rich and famous man," added a priest.

Judas said aloud, "I am contented," and added to himself, "Now the star of hope is rising for me."

Then said Caiaphas to the rabbi who sat below the judgment seat arrayed in blue velvet and gold, "Bring the thirty pieces of silver out of the treasury, and pay it over in the presence of the council."

"Is this your will?" he added, putting the question to the Sanhedrin.

A great shout went up of "Yes, yes, it is."

But some there were present who did not join in that cry. One of these, Nicodemus, stood up and asked the Sanhedrin, "How can you conclude so godless a bargain?" Then turning to Judas, he said, "And thou, abject wretch, dost thou not blush to sell thy Lord and master, thou God-forgetting traitor whom the earth shall swallow up? For thirty pieces of silver wouldst thou now sell that most loving friend and benefactor? O, pause while there is yet time. That blood-money will cry to heaven for vengeance, will burn like hot iron thy avaricious soul!"

Judas, surprised by this sudden outburst, stood trembling and amazed. Dathan, Caiaphas and the rest of the Sanhedrin displayed unmistakable indignation at this unexpected intervention on the part of Nicodemus.

Josue said: "Don't trouble yourself, Judas, about the speech of this zealot; let him go and be a follower of the false prophet. Thou dost thy duty as a disciple of Moses in serving the rightful authorities."

Then came in the rabbi with the silver in a dish. "Come, Judas," said he, "take the thirty pieces of silver and play the man," counting the coins out on a stone table so that they chinked merrily as they fell.

Judas snatched them up eagerly, testing them now and then to see if they were genuine, and then transferred them piece by piece with feverish haste to his bag, which he tied up when filled and replaced in his girdle. Then, resuming his place on the left of the judgment seat, he exclaimed: "You can rely upon my word."

"But," said the priests, "the work must be accomplished before the feast."

Judas answered and said: "Even now the fairest opportunity offers itself. This very night he shall be in your hands. Give me an armed band so that he can be duly surrounded and every road of escape cut off."

Then said Annas, who up to now had not broken silence: "Let us send with him the Temple Watch."

"Yes, yes," cried all the priests, "let us order them to go."

Caiaphas said: "It would also be advisable to send some members of the Holy Sanhedrin with them."

Half the assembly sprang to their feet crying: "We are ready."

Caiaphas said: "If the choice is left to me I appoint Nathan, Josaphat, Solomon and Ptolomaus." Each of the four, as he was named, rose and bowed low.

Then, Caiaphas, turning to Judas, said: "But, Judas, how will the band be able to distinguish the Master in the darkness?"

Judas answered: "They must come with torches and lanterns and I will give them a sign."

"Excellent, Judas," cried the priests in approving chorus.

"Now," said Judas, "I will hasten away to spy out everything. Then I will come back to fetch the armed men."

"I will go with you, Judas," said Dathan, "and will not leave your side until this work is finished."

"At the gate of Bethpage I will meet your people," said Judas, as he departed, taking with him Dathan and the four priests to accompany him.

When they had left the Sanhedrin Caiaphas addressed the assembly: "All goes admirably, venerable fathers, but now we are called to look the great question frankly in the face. What shall we do with this man when God has delivered him into our hands?"

Then: said Zadok: "Let us throw him into the deepest and darkest of dungeons and keep him well watched and laden down with chains. Let him be buried while still alive."

This, however, did not please Caiaphas, so using the full might of his eloquence and authority he continued: "Which of you would guarantee that his friends would not raise a tumult and free him, or that the guard might not be corrupted, or could he not break his fetters with his abhorred magic arts?" The priests were silent. Caiaphas replied in tones of the deepest conviction: "I see that ye neither know nor understand. Then listen to the high priest. It is better that one man should die and the whole nation perish not. He must die!" And as the fatal words fell from the lips of Caiaphas the whole Sanhedrin was moved. Caiaphas continued: "Until he is dead there is no peace in Israel, no security for the law of Moses, and no quiet hours for us."

Hardly had Caiaphas ended than the rabbi sprang to his feet exclaiming in excited tones: "God has spoken through our high priest! Only by the death of Jesus of Nazareth can and must the people of Israel be delivered!"

Nathanael exclaimed: "Long has the word lain upon my tongue! Now is it uttered. Let him die, the foe of our fathers!" Then sprang all the priests from their seats and with uplifted hands and eager voices exclaimed: "Yes, he must die; in his death is our salvation!" When they sat down, Annas, the aged high priest arose, and speaking with intense bitterness, declared: "By my gray hairs let it be sworn, I will never rest until our shame is washed out in the blood of this deceiver."

Then stood up Nicodemus and said: "O, fathers, is it allowed to say one word?" And all cried: "Yes, yes, speak, speak!" Then said Nicodemus: "Is the sentence already pronounced upon this man before there has been an examination or hearing of the witnesses? Is this a proceeding worthy of the fathers of the people of God?" Nathanael said: "What! Wilt thou accuse the council of injustice?" Zadok exclaimed: "Dost thou know the holy law? Compare——" Nicodemus replied: "I know the law; therefore also I know that the judge may not pass sentence before witnesses are heard." "What need we any further witnesses?" cried Josue. "We ourselves have often enough been witnesses to his speech and his actions, by which he blasphemously outraged the law." Nicodemus answered, unmoved by the clamor of the assembly: "Then you yourselves are at once the accusers, the witnesses and the judges. I have listened to his sublime teachings; I have seen his mighty deeds. They call for belief and admiration; not for contempt and punishment."

"What," exclaimed Caiaphas indignantly, "this scoundrel deserves admiration! Thou wilt cleave to Moses and yet defendest thou that which the law condemns? Ha! Fathers of Israel, the impious words call for vengeance."

The priests shouted: "Out with thee from our assembly, if thou persist in this way of speaking!" when another voice is heard.

Joseph of Arimathea stood forth on the opposite side of the hall and said: "I must also agree with Nicodemus. No one has imputed any deed to Jesus which makes him worthy of death; he has done nothing but good."

Then said Caiaphas: "Dost thou also speak in this wise? Is it not known everywhere how he desecrated the Sabbath; how he has misled the people by his seditious speeches? Hath he not also as a deceiver worked his pretended miracles by the aid of Beelzebub? Has he not given himself out as a God, when he is nothing but a man?"

"You hear that?" cried the priests to Joseph. He remained standing and continued saying: "Envy and malice have misrepresented his words and imputed evil motives to the noblest acts. That he is a man come from God his God-like acts testify."

"Ha," cried Nathanael, with a laugh of scorn, "now we know thee. Already for a long time hast thou been a secret follower of this Galilean! Now, thou hast shown thyself in thy true colors!"

Aged Annas, without leaving his seat, remarked: "So, then, we have in our very midst traitors to our holy law, and even here has the deceiver cast his net."

"What do ye here, apostates?" cried Caiaphas. "Be off to your prophet, to see him once more, before the hour strikes when he must die, for that is irrevocably determined."

"Yes," cried all the priests. "Yes! die he must; that is our resolve."

Then said Nicodemus, "I curse this resolution; I will neither have part nor lot in this shameful condemnation."

"And I also," said Joseph of Arimathea, "will quit this place where the innocent are condemned to death. By God, I swear that my hands are clean!"

Gathering their robes together, Nicodemus and Joseph of Arimathea walked slowly out of the Sanhedrin.

Then said Josue, "At last we are rid of these traitors. Now we can speak out freely." Caiaphas, however, profiting by the protests of Nicodemus and Joseph of Arimathea, said to the assembly: "It will certainly be necessary that we should sit formally in judgment upon this man, to try him and to bring forth witnesses against him, otherwise the people will believe that we have only persecuted him from envy and hatred."

Then said one Jacob, "Two witnesses at least the law requires," and Samuel answered: "These shall not be lacking; I will provide them myself."

Then said Dariabbas, "Our decision stands firm, but in order not to offend the weak it would be well to observe the usual forms of justice."

"And," added Ezekiel complacently, "should these forms not suffice the strength of our will we must supply what is lacking."

And a rabbi said, "A little more or less guilty matters little, since once for all the public weal demands that he should be removed."

Then Caiaphas said, "In securing the execution of our sentences it would be safest if we could so contrive that the sentence of death should be pronounced by the governor; then we should be clear of all responsibility."

"We can try," said Nathanael. "If it miscarries, it is still always open to us to have our sentence carried out by our trusty friends in the commotion of a great tumult, without ourselves being openly responsible for anything."

"And then," said the rabbi, "if the worst come we should have him in our hands, and in the silence of a dungeon it will not be difficult to find a more sure hand to deliver the Sanhedrin from its enemy."

Then Caiaphas arose and said, "Circumstances will teach us what should be done. Now let us break up. But hold yourselves ready at any hour of the night to be called together. There is no time to be lost. Our resolution is, he must die."

And all the members of the high council cried tumultuously: "Let him die! Let him die! The enemy of our holy land!"

CHAPTER IV

BETRAYED BY A KISS

The foulest deed will soon be done
That earth or hell displays—
Alas! ere this night's course be run
Judas his Lord betrays!

Come now, ye faithful souls draw nigh
See Jesus suffer, bleed and die,
Now has begun the anguished fight
Beyond in dark Gethsemane.
O, sinners never let this night
For evermore forgotten be!

For your salvation this has been
Which on the mountain we have seen,
When, sorrowing unto death, he sank
To earth, it was for you—
'Twas for your sake the damp turf drank
Those drops of crimson dew.

In the twilight of the same day there were gathered together in the neighborhood of the Mount of Olives those appointed by the Sanhedrin to seize Jesus. Judas was there with Dathan and the other traders, as well as the four priests sent by Caiaphas to see that all things went well. With them came the Temple Watch under the command of one Selpha, in steel helmet and steel-embossed leather cuirass. The watch consisted of twenty men in armor, two of whom carried long clubs set with spikes, two bore braziers of burning coals, while the rest carried spears. Conspicuous among the watch were Malchus, the high priest's servant, and Balbus. They approached stealthily, and Judas addressed them, saying, "Now be careful! We are now approaching the place whither the Master has withdrawn himself."

Then said Solomon, one of the priests, "I suppose the disciples will not perceive us too soon."

"No," said Judas, "they rest unconcerned and dream nothing of any attack. As to any resistance, there is nothing of that to fear."

Then cried the Temple Watch aloud, "Should they try it they shall feel the weight of our arms."

"You will seize him," said Judas, "without a single sword stroke."

"But," said Josue, "how shall we know him in the darkness so as not to arrest another in place of the one we desire?"

"I shall give you a sign," said Judas, "when we are in the garden; then look out. I will hasten up to him, and the man whom I shall kiss; that is he; bind him!"

Then said Korah, "Good, this sign will prevent us from making any mistake."

Ptolomaus, the priest, then turned to the watch and said, "Do you hear? You will know the master by a kiss!"

"Yes, yes," cried the soldiers, "we shall not miss him."

"Now," said Judas, "let us make haste; it is time. We are not far from the garden."

Then said Josue to Judas, "Judas, if tonight brings us good fortune, thou wilt profit by the fruit of thy work."

The traders added, "We, too, will recompense thee richly."

Then cried all the soldiers together, "Now look out, thou stirrer-up of the people, thou wilt soon have thy reward." Thereupon the whole company moved off into the darkness and remained hidden in an ambush until the signal should be given.

After a time Jesus and his disciples entered the garden of Gethsemane. Jesus spoke unto them, saying, "Verily, verily, I say unto you, ye shall weep and lament, but the world shall rejoice; ye shall be sorrowful, but your sorrow shall be turned into joy, for I will see you again and your heart shall rejoice, and your joy no one taketh from you. I came forth from the Father and am come into the world. I leave the world again and go unto the Father."

"Lo," said Peter, "now thou speakest plainly and no more in parables."

Then said James the Greater, "Now we see that thou knowest all things, and hast no need that one should ask thee anything."

And Thomas added, "Therefore we believe that thou comest forth from God."

Jesus answered them saying, "Do ye now believe? Behold the hour cometh, yea, is already come, when ye shall be scattered every man to his own and leave me alone. Yet I am not alone, for the Father is with me. Yes, Father, the hour is come; glorify thy Son that thy Son also may glorify thee. I have finished the work which thou hast given me to do. I have manifested thy name to those thou gavest me out of the world. Holy Father, keep them in thy name; sanctify them in the truth. Neither pray I for these alone, but for them also who shall believe on me through their word; that they may all be one, as thou, Father, art in me, and I in thee. Father, I will pray that they also whom thou hast given me be with me where I am, that they may behold my glory which thou hast given me, for thou lovedst me before the foundation of the world." Then turning to the disciples who were following him into the garden he said in a voice which was broken with sorrow: "Children, sit down here while I go and pray yonder. Pray that ye enter not into temptation; but you, Peter, James and John follow me." Eight of the disciples then sat down on the ground under the trees, while Jesus went forward with the three.

Bartholomew said, "Never have I seen him so sad;" and James the Less replied, "My heart is also laden down with sadness;" while Matthew cried, "Ah, that this night were passed with its weary hours." And another apostle exclaimed, "Not in vain has our master prepared us for this."

Philip said, "Dear brothers, we will sit down here and rest until he comes back."

"Yes," said Thomas, "that we will, for I am utterly worn out and weary."

Then Jesus, who had come forward with Peter, James and John, said unto them, "Ah, beloved children, my soul is exceeding sorrowful, even unto death. Tarry ye here and watch with me." Then after a pause he added, "I will go a little further apart in order to strengthen myself by communion with the Father."

As Jesus with slow and staggering steps went toward the grotto,

Peter cried, looking after him, "Ah, dear good master," and John exclaimed, "My soul is suffering with our teacher."

As they sat down Peter said, "I am very anxious."

James said, "Why does our dear master thus separate us from one another?"

John replied, "Alas, we are to be witnesses," and Peter continued, "Ye know, brethren, we were the witnesses of his transfiguration on the mountain, but now, what is it that we have to see?"

Slowly Peter, James and John, who were sitting apart, fell asleep.

Jesus having reached the grotto, said, "This hour must come upon me—the hour of darkness. For this it was that I came into the world." Then falling upon his knees he clasped his hands, and looking up to heaven cried, with a great and pitiful voice, "Father, my Father! If it be possible, and with thee all things are possible, let this cup pass from me!" Then Jesus fell upon his face on the ground and remained silent for a while. Then again he rose upon his knees and cried, "Yes, Father, not as I will, but as thou wilt!" Then standing up, he looked toward heaven and slowly returned to the three disciples.

And lo, when he approached he found them asleep. "Simon," he said.

Simon Peter, as in a dream, rubbed his head and said, "Alas, my master."

Jesus said, "Simon, dost thou sleep?"

Peter, rousing himself, said, "Master, here I am."

Jesus said, "Could you not watch with me one hour?"

Peter cried, "O, Master, forgive."

The apostles said, "Rabbi, sleep has overpowered us."

Then said Jesus, "Watch and pray that ye enter not into temptation."

The apostles answered, "Yes, Lord, we will watch and pray."

Then said Jesus unto them; "The spirit indeed is willing, but the flesh is weak." So saying he turned from them, and again slowly walked toward the grotto.

Praying he said, "My Father, thy demand is just, thy decrees are holy, thou claimest this sacrifice." Then falling upon his knees, he prayed, saying, "Father, the strife is hot." Falling upon his face he remained silent for a time, then raising himself again he cried, "Yes, Father, if this cup may not pass from me unless I drink it, Father thy will be done." Then standing up he said, "Holy One, it will be completed by me in righteousness."

Then once more he came back to his sleeping disciples; this time he did not rouse them.

"Are also your eyes so heavy that you could not watch?" he said. "Ah, my most trusted ones, even among you I find no consolation."

Then returning over the rocky road which led to the grotto he paused for a moment in sorrow, while a great sorrow overwhelmed him. "Oh, how dark it grows around me; the anguish of death encompasses me! The burden of God's judgment lies upon me! Oh, the sins! Oh, the sins of mankind! They weigh me down. Oh, the fearful burden; oh, the bitterness of this cup!" Then coming to the grotto again, he cried, "My Father!" and falling down he prayed, "If it is not possible that this hour pass away from me, thy will be done! Thy holiest will! Father! Thy son! Hear him!"

Then from out of the darkness a bright and shining angel in white apparel and with radiant wings descended upon him. And out of the silence were heard these words, "O, Son of Man, sanctify the Father's will! Look upon the blessedness which will proceed from thy struggles. The Father has laid it upon thee to become the sacrifice for sinful man. Carry it through to the end. The Father will glorify thee!"

Then said Jesus, "Yes, most Holy Father, I adore thy Providence; I will complete the work—to reconcile—to save, to bless!" Then standing up he cried in a more joyous tone, "Strengthened by thy word, O Father! I go joyfully to meet that to which thou hast called me, as the substitute for sinful man."

With lighter step he returned to the place where the three disciples lay slumbering peacefully. He looked upon them and said, "Sleep now and take your rest."

Peter, hearing his voice, said, "What is it, master?"

Then all three answered, "Behold, we are ready."

Then said Jesus, "The hour is come; the son of man is betrayed into the hands of sinners. Rise, let us be going."

Even as he spoke these words the tramp of armed men was heard in the immediate neighborhood of the garden mingled with loud cries of denunciation and vengeance.

"What is that uproar?" said the apostles.

"Come," said Philip, who hurried from behind with the rest of the eight, "Come, let us gather around the master." At that word the disciples hastened forward.

"Behold," said Jesus, "he who betrayeth me is at hand." The disciples looked in the direction which Jesus indicated, and there by the flaring light of the braziers carried by the Temple Watch, they saw Judas advancing at the head of his band.

"What does this multitude want?" said Andrew.

For an answer all the disciples cried as with one voice, "Alas! we are undone!"

"And see," cried John, "Judas is at their head."

Even as he said this, Judas, with long and stealthy steps, sprang forward, looking from side to side as he came, until he stopped immediately behind Jesus; then standing on tiptoe he reached over the shoulder of Jesus and kissed him, saying, "Hail, Master."

Jesus answered, "Friend, wherefore art thou come? Betrayest thou the son of man with a kiss?" Then stepping forward to meet the armed band, he faced them fearlessly and said, "Whom seek ye?"

A loud and angry shout went up from the soldiers: "Jesus of Nazareth!"

Jesus said, "I am he."

As he uttered these word the soldiers fell backward to the ground, crying, "Woe unto us! What is this?"

The disciples exultantly cried, "One single word from him casts them to the ground."

But Jesus said to the soldiers, "Fear not; arise."

As they regained their feet the disciples whispered eagerly to Jesus saying, "Lord, cast them down so that they shall never rise again."

But Jesus a second time asked, "Whom seek ye?"

Again the crowd replied, "Jesus of Nazareth."

Then Jesus said, "I have already told you that I am he; if therefore, ye seek me, let these go their way."

Selpha, the leader of the band, cried, "Seize him!" The soldiers approached Jesus, Malchus and Balbus carrying in their hands a small cord, and grasped him by the wrists in order to bind him.

Peter and Philip asked Jesus, saying, "Lord, shall we smite with the sword?" Before Jesus replied, Peter's sword flashed from its sheath and descended on the head of Malchus. The helmet turned the descending blade, and instead of splitting his skull it only sliced off his ear.

"Alas!" cried Malchus, "I am wounded; my ear is off."

Then said Jesus to the disciples, "Suffer ye thus far," and reaching forward to Malchus he said, "Be not troubled; thou shalt be healed." And touching his ear, that moment it was made whole. Malchus felt his ear with astonishment. His comrades satisfied themselves that the ear was as the other and stood motionless, while Jesus turned to Peter and said, "Put up thy sword into its sheath, for all they who take the sword shall perish with the sword. The cup which the Father hath given, shall I not drink it? Thinkest thou I cannot now pray to my Father, and he would presently give me more than twelve legions of angels? But how, then, would the Scriptures be fulfilled that thus it must be?" Then turning to the Pharisees he said, "Are ye come out as against a thief with swords and staves to take me? I sat daily with ye in the temple teaching, and ye took me not. But this is your hour and the power of darkness. Behold, I am here!"

"Surround him!" cried Selpha; "bind him fast that he escape not."

Then said Nathanael, whose eager zeal to destroy Jesus had led him to join the soldiers, "You are responsible to the council that he does not escape." At Selpha's command Malchus and Balbus had seized Christ, and were busily engaged in tying his hands together with cords. Slowly, one by one, the disciples stole away, leaving Jesus alone in the midst of his captors.

In reply to Nathanael, the soldiers said, "Out of our hands he will not escape."

Then cried with a loud voice the traders, with Dathan at their head, "Now, we will wreak our vengeance." And Dathan added, "Dost thou still remember what thou didst to us in the temple?"

Josaphat said to the other Pharisees, "We will hasten on into the city. The Sanhedrin will be awaiting our arrival with impatience."

The traders replied, "But we will not leave this scoundrel for an instant."

"First," said Nathanael, "we must go to the High Priest Annas. Lead him thither!"

Selpha said, "We follow thee!"

As the band prepared to obey the word of command a trader came up to Judas and said approvingly, "Thou art a man, indeed. Thou knowest how to keep thy word."

Judas complacently answered, "Did I not tell you that he would be in your power today?"

The Pharisees said, "Thou hast placed the whole council under an obligation to thee."

The procession then went off, leading Jesus to the palace of Annas. The Temple Watch formed behind Jesus, who with his hands bound before him, was thrown violently forward by Malchus and Balbus, who held the other ends of the cords which bound him, and marched behind him. They cried, "On with thee! In Jerusalem they will settle your affair!"

Selpha, who marched at the head of his band, cried, "Let us hasten; lead him away carefully."

And all the band shouted, "Ha, run now as thou hast hitherto run to and fro about the land of Judea."

"Spare him not!" said Selpha, "drive him on!"

"Forward," shouted the soldiers, shouting together; "otherwise thou shalt be driven on with staves."

And as they marched away, driving Jesus before them the traders derided him, saying, "Doth Beelzebub, then, aid thee no longer?"

It was dark night and there was silence in the street before the house of Annas, the high priest, when his door opened and Annas, attended by Esdras, Sidrach and Missel, came upon the balcony. "I can find no rest this night," said Annas, looking impatiently down the street, "until I know that this disturber of the peace is in our hands. Oh, if he were only safe, and in fetters. Full of longing and anxiety I await the arrival of my servants with the joyful news."

Then said Esdras, "They cannot be much longer, for it is a good while since they went away."

"In vain has my troubled gaze looked up and down the street of Kedron. But nothing can I see and nothing hear. Go, my Esdras, go toward the Kedron gate and see."

"I will hasten out," said Esdras, hurrying away as quickly as his short, squat figure would allow.

Annas, walking about impatiently, tormented by misgivings as to the success of the enterprise, began: "It would be a blow to the Sanhedrin if this time the work should not succeed."

Sidrach said, "Do not give away to anxiety, high priest," and Missel added, "There is no doubt of our success."

Annas, heeding not the consolation of his priests, said, "They may have altered their way and returned through the Siola Gate. I must send to see also on that side."

Sidrach said, "If the high priest wishes it I will go to the Siola Gate."

"Yes, do," said Annas, "but first see whether anyone comes through the street of the Sanhedrin."

"I will not loiter, my lord," said Sidrach, as he disappeared in the darkness.

Annas resumed his troubled thoughts. "The night is going by, and still the old uncertainty. Every minute of this weary waiting time is as an hour to me. Hark, I think some one comes running! Yes, he comes. Surely there will be good tidings."

Sidrach, bursting into the presence of the high priest, exclaimed, "My lord, Esdras comes in haste. I saw him just now running down the street with rapid foot."

Then said Annas, "Surely it is joyful news that he brings since he hastens so. Truly, I long for nothing now but the death of this malefactor."

Then came Esdras, breathless with haste, crying, "Hail to the high priest. I have seen the fathers who were sent to Judas. All has gone according to your wish. The Galilean is in bonds. I heard it from their mouth, and hurried as fast as I could to bring the joyful news in haste to thee."

Annas cried, "Oh, heavenly message! Auspicious hour! A stone is lifted from my heart; I feel as if I were born again. Now for the first time can I rejoice to call myself high priest of the chosen people."

Then came in to Annas, Judas and the four Pharisees, who had been sent by the council to accompany him, crying, "Long live our high priest!"

Nathanael exclaimed, "The wish of the council is accomplished."

Annas said, "Oh, I must embrace you for joy. So, then, our plan has succeeded. Judas, thy name shall take an honorable place in our annals. Even before the feast shall the Galilean die."

Judas, whom the Pharisees had brought in with the prisoner, startled by that word, sprang back, repeating incredulously, "Die!"

"His death is declared!" said Annas.

"For his life and blood," cried Judas, "I will not be responsible."

"That is unnecessary," said Annas coolly, "he is in our power."

"But," persisted Judas passionately, "I have not delivered him over to you for that."

"Thou hast delivered him over," said the Pharisees, "and the rest is our business."

Repulsed on every side, Judas, striking his forehead with his hand, cried, "Woe is me; what have I done? Shall he die? No! That I did not wish. That I will not have."

As he hurried into the street the Pharisees laughed at him and said, "Whether thou wilt have it or not, die he must."

Then said the priests to Annas, "High priest, the prisoner is at the threshold."

Annas said, "Let Selpha, with as many of the watch as are necessary, bring him up here, while the rest await him below." Then was Jesus brought before Annas on the balcony in custody with Selpha, the leader of the Temple Watch and the two servants of the temple, Malchus and Balbus, holding the cords by which Jesus was bound. The rest of the watch remained in the street below.

Selpha bowed low as he entered and said, "High priest, in accordance with thy command the prisoner now stands at thy bar."

When Annas saw Jesus he said, "Have you brought him alone as prisoner?"

Balbus answered, "His disciples dispersed like timid sheep."

Selpha said, "We did not find it worth the trouble to arrest them. Nevertheless Malchus almost lost his life."

"How did that happen?" asked Annas.

"One of his followers," said Selpha, "with a drawn sword smote him and cut off his ear."

"How could that be?" said Annas, looking first at one side of Malchus' head and then at the other. "It has left no mark; there is nothing to be seen."

"Oh," said Balbus, mocking, "the magician has conjured it back again."

"What sayest thou to that?" asked Annas. Malchus replied seriously, "I cannot explain it. It is a miracle that has happened to me."

Annas frowned, "Has the deceiver also bewitched thee?" he asked, and then turning to Jesus said to him, "Say, by what power hast thou done this?" Jesus did not answer.

"Speak," said Selpha, "when the high priest asks thee."

"Speak," said Annas. "Give an account of thy disciples and thy teaching, which thou hast spread abroad over the whole land of Judea and with which thou hast corrupted the people."

Then Jesus answered and said unto him, "I spake openly to the world, I ever taught in the synagogue and in the temple, and in secret I taught nothing. What askest thou me? Ask them that heard me what I have spoken. Behold, they know what I have said."

Balbus, who was standing on the left hand of Jesus holding one end of the cord by which his hands were bound, struck him over the face a resounding blow, saying, "Answerest thou the high priest so?"

Jesus answered, "If I have spoken evil, bear witness of the evil, but if I have spoken well why smitest thou me?"

Then Annas exclaimed, "Wilt thou even now defy us, when thy life and death are in our power? I am weary of this villain!" and gave the signal for Jesus to be removed.

"Oh," said Balbus, as he roughly thrust him forward, "wait a little. Thy obstinacy will vanish."

As Jesus was being led down the steps Annas exclaimed, "I will go in now for a little while to rest, or rather to meditate quietly as to how the work so happily begun may be brought to an end. In any case the summons to the Sanhedrin will reach me at an early hour in the morning." Annas then entered into his own house, leaving Jesus in the street below in the midst of the soldiers. As Selpha appeared bringing Jesus into the street the watch cried out loudly, "Ha, is this business already over?"

Selpha said, "His defense has turned out badly," and Balbus added, "After all it gained him a smart slap over the face."

Selpha said, "Take him now and away with him to the palace of Caiaphas."

"Off with him," cried the soldiers tumultuously.

"Lift up thy feet. Cheer up!" said Balbus, mocking, "Thou wilt have a still better reception from Caiaphas," and the soldiers shouted as they marched, "There will be the raven's croak about thine ears!"

When Jesus was taken from the house of Annas he was led through the streets, the band accompanying him, shouting as they went. On their way to the Sanhedrin they led Jesus down the street which passed Pilate's house, and as they went they cried to him with riotous laughter, "Thou shalt become a laughing stock for the whole nation!"

Balbus said unto him scoffingly, "Make haste! Thy disciples are quite ready to proclaim thee King of Israel."

And the soldiers laughed as they said, "Thou hast often dreamed of this; is it not so?"

Then said Selpha, "Caiaphas will soon explain this dream to him."

And Balbus, seeing that Jesus opened not his mouth, and was silent, shouted in his ear, "Dost thou hear? Caiaphas will announce to thee thy exaltation to a high position!"

A great burst of hoarse laughter from the watch followed, as they shouted, "An exalted position between heaven and earth!"

"Look out, you fellows!" cried Selpha, "there through the hall of Pilate's lies our nearest way to the palace of Caiaphas. There, station yourselves in the courtyard until further orders."

The soldiers answered, "Thy command shall be fully obeyed!"

Hardly had the noisy soldiery passed with their prisoner out of the street than Peter and John appeared before the house of Annas. Then said Peter, "How will it fare here with our good master? Oh, John, how anxious I am about him!"

John answered, "He is certain to have to suffer here scorn and ill treatment. I am very much afraid of approaching the house."

Peter said, "But it is so silent about here."

John replied, "One hears not a sound in the place. Could they have taken him away again?"

As they were talking Esdras came out from the house of Annas and asked, "What do you want at the palace at this time of night?"

John answered, "Forgive us; we saw a number of people from afar come hither from the Kedron Gate, and we came here in order to see what had happened."

Esdras answered, "They have brought in a prisoner, but he has already been sent to Caiaphas."

"To Caiaphas," said the disciples, "then we will go away at once."

"You had better, otherwise I will have you taken, up as night brawlers," said Esdras.

"We will go away quietly and make no disturbance," said Peter, meekly.

As they went the priest, looking after them, said, "Perhaps they are followers of the Galilean. If I only knew. However, they will not escape our people if they go to the palace of Caiaphas. The whole of his following must be destroyed. Otherwise the people will never be brought into obedience." He then returned into the house.

CHAPTER V

PETER COMMITS PERJURY

> How bleeds my heart!
> The Holiest stands before the judgement seat.
> The malice of sinners he must bear,
> Betrayed and outraged, bound and beaten there.
> O, sons of men, your faces veil this day!—
> The scarred form is touched by impious hands,
> From Annas dragged to Caiaphas away,
> What's here foreshadowed, see, fulfilled it stands.
> See Jesus, how in silence he
> Bears outrage, blows and mockery!
> O! what a man!
> Oh, hearts of men who now draw near,
> Melt with compassion when you see
> Bowed down in deepest misery!
> O! what a man!

Caiaphas, in his bed chamber, wearing a dressing gown, surrounded by priests, exulted over the news which had been brought him of the arrest of Jesus.

"This happy capture," said he, "promises us a fortunate realization of our wishes. I thank you, noble members of the Sanhedrin, for zealous and prudent co-operation."

But the priests with one voice cried, "The greatest share of praise belongs to our high priest!"

"Now," said Caiaphas, "let us pursue our path without delay. Everything is ready! The council will immediately be assembled. The necessary witnesses have already been brought along. I shall now without losing a moment, at once begin the trial of the prisoner. Then judgment shall be pronounced and provision made that it shall be executed. The quicker the execution the surer the result!"

Dathan said, "It would be advisable to get everything over before our adversaries recover their senses."

Caiaphas replied, "I have encountered this necessity. Trust me, my friends. I have thought of a plan. I hope to carry it out."

At this Zadok said, "The wisdom of our high priest deserves our fullest confidence," and then cried they all, "the God of our fathers bless all his measures!"

Then Selpha, the leader of the band, brought Jesus into the chamber of Caiaphas, the high priest, Balbus and Malchus holding the cords by which his hands were bound.

"Illustrious High Priest, here is the prisoner," said Selpha.

"Bring him nearer," said Caiaphas, "so that I may look him in the face and question him."

"Step forward," said Selpha, "and show respect here to the head of the Sanhedrin."

Then Caiaphas, having looked into the face of Jesus, said to him disdainfully, "Thou art he then who dreamed of bringing about the destruction of the synagogue, and the law of Moses?" Then assuming a more judicial tone, he said, "Thou art accused that thou hast stirred up the people to disobedience, that thou hast despised the holy traditions of the fathers, that thou hast transgressed the divine command for the keeping of the Sabbath day, and that thou hast even been guilty of many blasphemous speeches and acts. Here," Caiaphas continues, pointing to five Jews who had entered the chamber at the same time as Selpha brought in Jesus, and had taken their stand on the left of the high priest, confronting the accused, "Here stand honorable men who are prepared to prove the truth, of these accusations by their testimony. Hear them and then thou mayest answer if thou canst."

Then stood forth the first witness and spoke, saying, "I can testify before God that this man has stirred up the people by openly denouncing the members of the council and the scribes as hypocrites, ravening wolves in sheeps' clothing, blind leaders of the blind, and has declared that no one shall follow their work." At this the members of the Sanhedrin smiled approvingly one to another.

The second witness said, "I can also testify to this, and can still further declare that he has forbidden the people to pay tribute to Caesar."

"Yes," interrupted the first witness, "at any rate he has dropped words of double meaning about that."

Then Caiaphas turned to Jesus and said, "What sayest thou unto this?" He paused for a reply, but Jesus opened not his mouth. Then said Caiaphas, "Art thou silent? Hast thou nothing to answer?" But Jesus never answered a word.

The third witness took up his testimony. "I have often seen how he with his disciples, in defiance of the law, has eaten with unwashed hands; how he has become accustomed to hold friendly intercourse with publicans and sinners and go into their houses to eat with them."

"That we have also seen," cried the other witnesses together. "I have heard many credible people say that he has even spoken with Samaritans, and indeed has lived with them for days together."

Then the first witness began to speak again: "I was a witness how he has done on the Sabbath what is forbidden by God's law, in that he healed sick and infirm people without fear on that day. He has seduced others to break the Sabbath; he ordered a man to take up his bed and carry it to his house." The second witness joined in, "I also can testify to this."

Again Caiaphas turned to Jesus and said, "What has thou to say against this evidence?" And after a pause, seeing that Jesus still spoke not, he said, "Hast thou nothing to say in reply?" But Jesus spoke not.

Then said the third witness, addressing himself to Jesus, "Thou hast, for I was present, taken upon thyself to forgive sins, which belongs to God alone. Thou hast, therefore, blasphemed God."

Then again spoke the first witness, "Thou hast called God thy Father, and hast dared to declare that thou art one with the Father. Thou hast therefore made thyself equal to God."

The second witness added, "Thou hast exalted thyself above our father Abraham. Thou didst say, 'Before Abraham was, I am.'"

Then spoke the fourth witness, who said, "Thou hast said, 'I can destroy the temple of God, and in three days build it up again.'"

The fifth witness, who had not hitherto spoken, stood forward and said, "I have heard thee say, 'I will destroy this temple which is made with hands, and in three days I will build another made without hands.'" This concluded the testimony of the witnesses.

Then Caiaphas, turning to Jesus, spoke to him with indignation: "So thou hast claimed to possess a superhuman divine power? These are serious accusations, and they are legally proved; answer if thou canst." Jesus remaining silent, Caiaphas resumed, "Thou thinkest that by silence thou canst save thyself. Thou darest not to admit before the fathers and judges of the people what thou hast taught before the people. Or dost thou dare?" Then rising to his utmost height, and stretching his hand on high, Caiaphas continued, "Hear, then, I, the high priest, adjure thee by the living God. Say—art thou the Messiah, the Son of the Most High?" and as he uttered the sacred name Caiaphas crossed his arms and dropped his head on his breast.

For a moment there was silence, then Jesus answered and said, "Thou hast said it, and so I am. Nevertheless, I say unto you, hereafter ye shall see the Son of Man sitting on the right hand of God in power and coming in the clouds of heaven."

As Jesus spoke these words, the members of the council started in horror, and Caiaphas rending his robe, exclaimed with a loud voice, "He has blasphemed God! What need have we of any further witnesses? You yourselves have heard the blasphemy. What think ye?"

And all the members of the council cried together, "He is worthy of death."

Then said Caiaphas, "He is thus unanimously declared worthy of death. But not I, not the council, but the law of God pronounces the death sentence upon him. You teachers of the law, I call upon you to answer; what does the holy law say of him who is guilty of disobedience to the authorities appointed by God?" Then stood up Josue, and unrolling the book of the law read therefrom: "The man that will do presumptuously and will not hearken to the priest that standest to minister there before the Lord thy God, or unto the judge, even that man shalt die, and thou shalt put away the evil from Israel."

Then again said Caiaphas, "What does the law decree concerning him who profaneth the Sabbath?"

Then Ezekiel stood up and read, "Ye shall keep the Sabbath therefore, for it is holy unto you. Every one that defileth it shall surely be put to death; for whosoever doeth any work therein that soul shall be cut off from his people."

Then asked Caiaphas, "How does the law punish the blasphemer?"

Then stood up Nathanael, and unrolling the book of the law, read: "Speak unto the children of Israel saying, whosoever curseth his God shall bear his sin. And he that blasphemeth the name of the Lord he shall surely be put to death; all the congregation shall certainly stone him, as well the stranger as him that is born in this land."

"Thus," said Caiaphas, "is the judgment pronounced upon this Jesus of Nazareth—pronounced according to law, and shall be carried out as speedily as possible. Meanwhile I will have the condemned placed under safe guard. Lead him forth, guard him, and by the safe dawn of the morning bring him to the Great Sanhedrin."

"Come, then, Messiah," said Selpha, roughly, "we will show thee thy palace."

"There thou shalt receive due homage," said Balbus, as he placed his hand on the shoulder of Jesus, and marched him out of the chamber.

Then said Caiaphas exultingly, "We are approaching the goal. Now, however, resolute steps are necessary."

The priests and Pharisees cried together, "We will not rest until he is brought to death."

Then said Caiaphas, "With the break of day let us come together again. This must be announced to the High Priest Annas and the rest. Then shall the sentence be confirmed by the whole assembled council, and the prisoner will immediately be brought before Pilate in order that he may confirm it and have it executed."

The priests then departed, crying as they went, "God deliver us soon from our enemy."

When the council had been dismissed and all was still, Judas, moving as one distracted, came down the street in front of the high priest's palace; as he went he muttered to himself: "Fearful forebodings drive me hither and thither. That word of Annas' 'He must die!' Oh, that word pursues me everywhere." Then, as if he remembered all that had happened, Judas cried, "No, it cannot come to that; they will not carry things so far! That would be too terrible if my Master—no!—and I—guilty of it? No! Here in the house of Caiaphas, I will inquire how things stand. Shall I go in? I can no longer bear this uncertainty, and it terrifies me to ascertain the certainty. My heart throbs with terror—surely I shall not have to hear the worst. Yet it must come some time." And thereupon he went into the house of the high priest.

Meanwhile in the hall of Caiaphas the Temple Watch was standing waiting the result of the examination of Jesus before Caiaphas. In the hall were the servant maids, Sarah and Hagar, who seeing the soldiers standing outside, went to the door, and said, "You may come in here." It was Hagar who spoke first, and Sarah added, "It is more comfortable in here."

"True for you, good people," said Melchi, one of the soldiers. Then calling out, "Ho, comrades, come in! It is better for us to lie down in the hall."

Then said a soldier named Arphaxad, "I like this; I wish we had come in long ago; how stupid we are, always standing outside in the open air and shivering. But where is there any fire?"

"Sarah," added another soldier, "go and bring us fire, also wood to lay thereon."

"Willingly," said Hagar.

"That you shall have," said Sarah. They went out together to comply with the soldier's wish.

"Will the trial soon come to an end?" asked several of the soldiers.

"It will last," said Melchi, "until all the witnesses are examined."

"And," added Panther, "the accused will also use all his eloquence to get himself out of the scrape."

"That will help him nothing," said Arphaxad; "he has offended the priests too much." Then returned the serving maids with a brazier in which there was a little fire and some wood, which they placed thereon, making a great smoke.

"Here is your fire," said Hagar, "wood and fire tongs."

Then cried the soldiers together, "Thanks, you good girls."

"Yes," said Panther, stooping down over the brazier, "that is good. Now take care that the fire does not go out." Several of the soldiers stooped over the fire, piled on wood, and Sarah busied herself with bringing in meat and bread.

Peter and John, who had been wandering about the streets seeking for tidings, came to the door, John preceding Peter. Hagar, who saw John standing in the entrance of the door, said, "John, comest thou also hither in the middle of the night? Come in here, then, thou must warm thyself. Could you make a little room for this young man here?" said Hagar addressing the soldiers.

"Yes, indeed," cried the band together.

Then said John, "Good Hagar, I have a companion with me; can he not also come in?"

"Where is he?" said Hagar. "Let him come in; why does he stand out in the cold?"

John went to where Peter was standing, but came back alone.

"Where is he?" said Hagar.

"He stands on the threshold, but does not trust himself to come in," replied John.

Then Hagar went to the door and said, "Come in, good friend; do not be afraid."

All the soldiers cried, "Friend, come also in here to us and warm thyself!" Peter without saying a word timidly drew near to the fire and warmed his hands in the smoke.

The men went on talking round the fire and Arphaxad said, after a pause, "We still see and hear nothing of the prisoner."

Several then asked together, "How much longer must we wait here?"

Then said Panther, "Probably he will come out from the trial as a man condemned to death."

"I wonder," said Arphaxad, "whether his disciples will be sought after?"

Peter trembled as the band with hoarse laughter cried aloud, "That would be a fine piece of work if they all had to be captured!"

Then said Panther, "It would not be worth the trouble. If the Master is once out of the way, then the Galileans will fly and never let themselves be seen again in Jerusalem. But," said Panther, "one at least ought to receive sharp punishment; he who in the garden drew his sword and cut off Malchus' ear."

"Yes, yes," cried the band, laughing, "that should be, as it is said, an ear for an ear!"

"Ha, ha, ha, a good idea!" laughed Panther, "but that rule would here find no application, for Malchus has his ear back again."

During this time, while the soldiers were laughing and talking, Hagar was curiously looking at Peter. Immediately a pause took place, Hagar said to Peter, "I have been observing thee for some time. Now, if I do not mistake, thou art one of the disciples of the Galilean. Yes, yes, thou wert with Jesus of Nazareth."

Peter started up from the fire over which he had been warming his hands and stammered out, "I? No, I am not. Woman, I know him not, neither know I what thou sayest."

When Hagar thus spoke all the soldiers looked at Peter, who fearing his attack on Malchus might be resented, tried to slip through the band and escape unobserved. Passing the fire, he came close to the other waiting maid, Sarah, who, looking him full in the face, said in a shrill voice, "See, this man was also with Jesus of Nazareth."

The attention of the whole band being aroused, they all clustered around Peter, asking, "Art thou also one of the disciples?"

Levi said, "Thou art one of them, quite certainly."

Peter in the midst of armed and violent men, looked confusedly from side to side and declared, "Upon my soul—I am not—I do not know the man."

Even as he spoke the cock crew, but the rattle of the weapons of the soldiers and imminent menace of a violent death left him no leisure to attend to anything but his own safety, for a soldier at the same moment exclaimed, "Look at this man. Of a truth he was also with him."

Then said Peter stoutly, "I know not what ye have to do with me. What does this man matter to me?"

But the soldiers crowding round him said, "Yes, yes, thou art one of them. Thou art also a Galilean; thy speech betrayeth thee."

Then Peter, raising his hands on high, said with a troubled voice, "God be my witness that I do not know the man of whom ye speak;" and the cock crew a second time.

Then Melchi, pressing forward, looked Peter full in the face and said, "Did I not see thee in the garden with him, when my cousin Malchus had his ear cut off?"

At this moment, when the situation was getting very serious for Peter, attention was called off from him by a cry from the soldiers round the fire. "Make ready, they are bringing in the prisoner." Selpha then brought in Jesus bound between Malchus and Balbus.

"Now, how have things gone?" eagerly inquired Arphaxad.

"He is condemned to death," said Selpha.

The soldiers mocking, cried, "Poor king!"

At this moment Jesus met Peter, and looked upon him with a gaze full of sorrow. Peter smote his head with his hand and went out into the night.

"Come," said Arphaxad, "he will help us to pass the time."

"Forward, comrades," said Selpha, "we must guard him till morning." Thereupon they all went out.

Peter, when he had left the hall of the high priest, went out into the street weeping bitterly and suffering anguish of soul. "Oh, my Master," he cried, "how deeply have I fallen! Oh, woe unto me, weak and wretched man! I have three times denied my dearest friend and teacher. I cannot understand how I could so forget myself. A curse upon my shameful faithlessness! How my heart will repent of it—this contemptible cowardice. My dearest Lord, hast thou still grace for me—grace for a faithless, one—oh! send it me! This once more hear the voice of my repentant heart. Alas! the sin is committed. I cannot undo it, but ever, ever, will I weep for it and repent of it—and now nevermore will I leave thee! Oh, thou most loving one! Thou wilt surely not cast me off! Thou wilt not despise my bitter, repentance. No! the gentle pitying look which thou didst cast upon thy deeply fallen disciple promises it—thou wilt forgive me. I have this hope from thee, best of teachers, and the whole love of my heart shall from this moment be given to thee. I will cling closely to thee and nothing, nothing shall ever be able to separate thee from me again!"

And with a face beaming with hope of forgiveness, even for his threefold denial, he went away.

Hardly had he gone, when John entered at the other end of the street, asking anxiously, looking on either side, "Where, then, can Peter have gone? In vain my eyes have sought him in the crowd. Surely nothing evil can have befallen him. Perhaps I still may meet him upon the road. I will now go to Bethany. Dearest mother, if I bring thee the tidings of these terrible things which have happened—the innocent one ill-treated and condemned by sinners, what wilt thy heart feel? O, Judas, Judas, what hast thou done?"

Now it came to pass that the soldiers having taken Jesus into the guardroom of Caiaphas' palace, mocked him and despitefully used him until it was day. They seated him on a stool with a bandage over his eyes, and surrounded him mockingly, saying, "Is not this throne too mean for thee, great king? Hail to thee, thou new-born sovereign! But sit more firmly," said one, seizing Jesus from behind and pressing him down on his chair. "Thou mightest otherwise fall down. Thou art verily also a prophet. So say, O great Elias, say who it is who has struck thee," and with that he dealt Jesus a blow on the face.

Others came in and also struck him, saying, "Was it I?" but Jesus answered nothing.

Then one of the band went up to him and shouted, "Hearest thou nothing?" and shook him violently by the shoulders. "Art thou asleep?" Then turning to his comrades he exclaimed, "He is deaf and dumb; a fine prophet indeed." And thereupon he roughly pushed Jesus forward so that he fell from the stool upon the ground upon his face.

"Alas! alas!" they cried. "Our king has fallen from his throne. What is to be done now? We have no longer any king. Thou art to be pitied, such a great magician and now so weak and weary! Come, help us to put him again upon his throne."

And then they seized him where he lay on the ground with his eyes bandaged and his hands tied, and lifted him again upon his seat. "Raise thyself, O mighty king; receive anew our homage."

As they were kneeling around him in scorn a messenger of Caiaphas entered saying, "How goes it now with the king?" and the band shouted, "He speaks and prophesies not; we can do nothing with him."

"Then," said the messenger, "the high priest and Pilate will soon make him speak. Caiaphas sends me to bring him."

"Up, comrades," said Selpha.

Thereupon, taking Jesus again by the cords which bound his hands, they led him off, saying, "Stand up; thou hast been king long enough." And all shouted, "Away with thee. Thy kingdom has come to an end."

CHAPTER VI

JUDAS HANGS HIMSELF

> The guilty deed fails not to win its wages,
> The guiltless blood he sold cries from the ground;
> Driven to madness by the worm that rages
> And scourged by furies, Judas ranges round
>   Wildly, and finds no rest
>   From the fire in his breast,
> Till swept away by bitterest despair
> He flings away in reckless haste
> The load of life he can no longer bear.

When Jesus was being mocked and ill-treated by the soldiers in the guardroom of Caiaphas' palace, Judas wandered to and fro in despair. "Now my fearful foreboding has become a terrible certainty. Caiaphas has sentenced the Master to death, and the council has concurred in his sentence. All is over. There is no hope, no way of escape. Had the Master wished to save himself he would have made them feel his might a second time in the garden. As he did not do it then, he will now do so no more. What can I do for him, I, a miserable wretch who have delivered him into their hands? They shall have the money back, that blood money. They must give me my Master back again. I will go at once and make the demand. But, oh, will he be saved by that? Oh, vain, foolish hope. They will mock me, I know it. O cursed synagogue, thou hast tempted me through thy messengers, thou hast hidden from me thy bloody designs until thou hadst him in thy clutches. I will torture thee with bitter reproaches, ye unjust judges. I will have nothing to do with your devilish decision. I will have no share in the blood of this innocent. Oh, what tortures, what pains of hell, tear my inmost soul!" So saying he departed.

Now within the hall of the Sanhedrin were assembled the high priests, the scribes and the leaders. Caiaphas and Annas arrayed in their robes, sat in the high place of the council, and all the seats were filled except those of Joseph of Arimathea and Nicodemus.

Caiaphas spoke, saying, "I thought, fathers, that I could not wait till the morning to send the enemy of the synagogue to death."

And Annas said, "I could not get a moment's rest for eagerness to hear the sentence pronounced."

Then cried they all, "It is pronounced. He shall and must die."

Caiaphas said, "I did not wish to trouble all the members of the Sanhedrin to come hither in the night time. But there was present the necessary number of judges to pronounce as the law prescribes. All as with one mouth declared the accused worthy of death, for all had heard with their own ears how this man blasphemed God in the most terrible way, and was impious enough to call himself the Son of God."

The priests and Pharisees who had previously been present answered, "Yea, we bear witness to it. We have ourselves heard the impious blasphemy from his lips."

"Then," said Caiaphas, "I will have the criminal brought before you once more, so that you may be convinced of his being worthy of death. Then may the whole council pronounce the just sentence."

As he was speaking, Judas, looking haggard and distracted, rushed into the midst of the council, crying wildly, "Is it true? Have you condemned my Master to death?"

Then said the rabbi unto him, "Why dost thou force thyself uncalled for in this assembly? Be off. We will call thee if we have need of thee."

But Judas took no heed. "I must know it," he said. "Have you condemned him?"

Then all in the council cried aloud, "He must die."

"Woe, woe!" said Judas. "I have sinned. I have betrayed innocent blood. Oh, you blood-thirsty judges, to condemn the innocent blood."

"Peace, peace, Judas," cried the council.

"There will never, never more be peace for me," said Judas, bitterly, "and none for you. The blood of the innocent cries aloud for vengeance."

"What has driven you crazy? Speak, but speak with reverence—thou standest before the Sanhedrin," said Caiaphas.

Then said Judas passionately: "You are determined to deliver him up to death; him who is free from all guilt. You must not do it. I have a protest to make against it. You have made me a traitor. Your accursed pieces of silver!"

Annas interrupted him, saying, "Thou didst propose it thyself and close the bargain."

Then said the priest unto him, "Recollect thyself, Judas, thou hast received what thou didst desire; and if thou behavest thyself decently thou canst still——"

Judas interrupted him. "I will have nothing more. I tear up your shameful bargain. Let the innocent go."

"Be off, madman," said a rabbi angrily.

But Judas, taking no heed, knelt and stretched his hands toward Caiaphas. "I demand the release of the innocent. My hands shall be free from his blood."

"What," said the rabbi, "thou contemptible traitor, wilt thou dictate to the Sanhedrin? Know this, thy Master must die, and thou hast delivered him to death."

And all the priests and Pharisees cried aloud, "He must die."

And Judas, with staring eyes, as one demented, repeated, "Die? Then I am a traitor. I have given him up to death!" He sank down like a man crushed by a blow, and then springing up and breaking out into wild passion, he shouted aloud: "May ten thousand devils from hell tear me in pieces! Let them grind me to powder! Here, ye bloodhounds, take your accursed blood money!" And with that he snatched the bag from his girdle and flung it violently before the seat of the high priest.

"Why didst thou let thyself be made the tool for a transaction which thou didst not weigh beforehand?" said Caiaphas.

"Yes," cried several, "it is your own business."

Then shouted Judas wildly, "May my soul be damned, my body burnt asunder, and ye—"

"Silence and out from here," cried all the priests together.

"And you," shouted Judas, above them all, "you will sink with me into the lowest hell!" He then rushed from the hall.

After a pause, during which the chief priests and rulers looked at each other in silence, the money lay unnoticed on the floor. Caiaphas said, "What a fearful man!"

"I had some foreboding of this," said Annas.

"It is his own fault," remarked a priest.

Then said Caiaphas, "Let him expiate that fault himself. He has betrayed his friend, we pursue our enemy. I remain steadfast by my determination, and if anyone here should be of another opinion, let him stand up."

"No," cried they all with one voice, "what has been resolved upon, let it be carried out."

Then said Caiaphas, "What shall we do with this money? It is blood money; it can no longer be put into the treasury of God."

Annas said, "It might be used for some useful purpose under the sanction of the high council."

All agreed to this, and a priest said, "A burying place for strangers is much wanted. With this money a field may be purchased for that purpose."

"Is there such a one in the market?" asked Caiaphas.

"Yes," said a priest, "a potter in the city has offered a piece of ground for sale at just this price."

"Let Saras conclude the purchase," said Caiaphas. They then picked up the money which had lain untouched on the floor.

"But now we will no longer delay to pronounce the capital sentence upon the prisoner," continued Caiaphas.

Then said a rabbi, "I will have him brought in at once."

"I shall see," said Annas, "whether the scorn which he showed toward me has not yet left him. A real satisfaction will it be to me to share in the sentence. Let him die."

Jesus then was brought in a second time before Caiaphas. Selpha, as before, preceded him, and Balbus and Malchus led him bound by the hands with a cord.

"Stand there," said Selpha, "and show more respect to the council than thou didst before." Then he added, "Venerable fathers, here we bring the prisoner."

Then said Caiaphas, "Lead him into the middle."

Balbus, laying his hand on the shoulder of Jesus, thrust him forward saying, "Step forward."

Then Caiaphas spake unto Jesus, saying, "Jesus of Nazareth, dost thou stand by the words which thou hast pronounced this night before thy judges?"

Annas added, "If thou be the Christ, tell us!"

Then Jesus answered and said, "If I tell you ye will not believe; if I also ask you, ye will not answer me nor let me go. But hereafter shall ye see the Son of Man sitting on the right hand of Almighty God." A shudder ran through the Sanhedrin, and all cried excitedly, "Art thou the Son of God?"

Jesus answered, "Ye say it and so I am."

Annas exclaimed, "It is enough; what need have we of any further witnesses?"

The priests and Pharisees who had not attended the night council, said, "We have now heard it out of his own mouth."

Then said Caiaphas, "Fathers of the people of Israel, it is now your duty to come to a final decision as to the guilt and punishment of this man."

Then cried they all, "He is guilty of blasphemy. He hath deserved death."

Caiaphas said, "We will therefore lead him before the judgment seat of Pilate."

And they all answered and said, "Yes, away with him. Let him die."

"Pilate," said Caiaphas, "must first be informed in order that he may proclaim the sentence before the feast."

A rabbi said, "Could some one be sent from the council in order to give him timely information?"

"Thou thyself," said Caiaphas, "together with Dariabbas and Rabinth shalt go before. We will speedily come after."

When these three had departed Caiaphas said, "This day, then, will save the religion of our fathers, and exalt the honor of the synagogue, so that the echo of our fame shall reach our latest descendants."

All shouted, "Men will speak of us centuries hence!" and Caiaphas resumed, "Lead him away; we follow."

Once more they cried, "Down with the Galilean!" and departed.

The three messengers sent by the Sanhedrin drew near to the house of Pilate, and as they went they spoke among themselves. The rabbi said: "At last we breathe more freely again; we have been insulted long enough."

Dariabbas replied, "It was indeed high time; his following was becoming very large."

"Now," said the rabbi, "there is nothing more to be feared from him. The traders have in these days displayed the most creditable activity, to have gained for us a crowd of determined people. You will see if it comes to anything, they will effectively take the lead. The waverers will concur with them, and the followers of the Nazarene will find it well to be silent, and take themselves off."

Then said Rabinth, seeing they had approached the place of Pilate, "How shall we bring our message to Pilate? We dare not enter the house of the Gentile today, as in that case we should become unclean and could not eat the Passover?"

"We will send a message through one of his own people," said the rabbi, and going up the stairs to the balcony of Pilate's house, he knocked gently at the door.

Standing and listening, he said, "Surely, there is some one there? Yes, there is some one coming," and retired a little way down the steps, so as to avoid any contact with the Gentile.

A servant of Pilate opened it and said, "Welcome, rabbi, will you not come in?"

"The precepts of the law will not allow us so to do today," said the rabbi.

The servant said, "Is that so? Can I carry your message?"

"The high priest sends us to bring a petition to the viceroy of Caesar to ask if he will allow the council to appear before him and to bring before him a malefactor for the confirmation of his sentence."

"I will deliver the message at once to my lord; wait here in the meantime," said the servant, and went into Pilate.

The rabbi returning down the steps joined Dariabbas and Rabinth, who stood below. "It is very sad," said Dariabbas, "that we must knock at the door of a Gentile in order to get the behests of our holy law executed."

"Take courage," said the rabbi, "when once this domestic enemy is removed out of the way, who knows whether we might not soon free ourselves from the foreign foe?"

Rabinth exclaimed, "Oh, may I live to see the day which will bring freedom to the children of Israel!"

Pilate's servant returned and spoke unto them saying, "The governor greets you. You are to inform the high priest that Pilate is ready to receive the petition of the Sanhedrin."

"Accept our thanks for thy kindness," said the rabbi. "Now let us hasten to report to the high priest the result of our errand." The servant then returned and closed the door behind him.

The three messengers then returned. Rabinth remarked anxiously, "Pilate will surely agree to the demand of the council."

"He must," said the rabbi, "how could he resist it when the Sanhedrin and the whole people demand with one voice the death of this man?"

"And besides," said Dariabbas, "what does the governor care about the life of a single Galilean? Were it merely to please the high priest, who is of great importance to him, he would not hesitate to permit the execution."

Now, Judas, being distracted by remorse, found himself, after wandering to and fro, in the potter's field, purchased with the thirty pieces of silver, in the midst of which stood a blasted tree. Then after wildly looking around to see if anyone was near, he said: "Oh, where, where can I go to hide my shame, to escape the torments of conscience? No forest is dark enough! No rocky cavern deep enough! O, earth, open and swallow me up! I can no longer exist. O, my dear Master! Him, best of all men, have I sold, giving him up to ill treatment, to a most painful death of torture. I, detestable betrayer—oh! where is there another man on whom such guilt of blood doth rest? Alas! nevermore can I appear before the face of the brethren. An outcast, hated and abhorred everywhere—branded as a traitor by those who led me astray—I wander about alone with this burning fire in my heart. There is still one left. Oh! might I look on the Master's face once more, I would cling to him as my only anchor. But he lies in prison, has perhaps been already slain by the rage of his enemies, although by my guilt, by my fault. I am the abhorred one who has brought him to prison and to death. Woe to me, the scum of men! There is no hope for me, my crimes can be expiated by no penance. For he is dead—and I, I am his murderer! Thrice unhappy hour in which my mother gave me to the world! Must I still drag on this life of agony and bear these tortures about with me?—as one pest stricken, flee from men, and be despised and shunned by all the world? No! I can bear it no longer! Not one step further! Here, O life accursed, here will I end thee! On these branches let the most disastrous fruit hang!" He untwined his girdle and twined it about his neck. "Ha, ha! come, thou serpent, entwine my neck and strangle the betrayer!"

As Judas spoke the last words he tied with convulsive and feverish agony the long girdle around his neck, fastened it to the branch of the tree, and swung himself off.

CHAPTER VII

JESUS, PILATE AND HEROD

    Thus before Pilate's judgment seat
    The council, full of passion's heat,
    Come to demand Messiah's blood.
    Oh, what has made them mad and blind?
    And what has kindled in their mind
        Of fury such a fiery flood?

    'Tis envy which no mercy knows
   In which hell's flame most fiercely glows—
      Lights this devouring fire,
    All's sacrificed unto its lust—
    Nothing too sacred, good or just
      To fall to its desire.
   Oh, woe to those whom passion sweeps
   Helpless and bound into the deeps.

Then went the high priests and the scribes, together with the rulers and traders of the temple, and the witnesses, to the house of Pilate. Jesus was led forth in front of them by Balbus and Malchus as before, Selpha being in command of the band of soldiers. As they went the soldiers shouted aloud, "Away with thee to death, thou false prophet! Ha! doth it dismay thee that thou wilt not go forward?"

"Drive him on," said Selpha. But Jesus being weary walked with slow footsteps.

Then the soldiers thrust him forward, crying, "Shall we have to carry thee in our arms? Go on! Thou hast not far to go, only to Calvary; there upon the cross thou canst rest in comfort."

By this time they had approached the precincts of Pilate's house. Then said Caiaphas to the soldiers, "Be still; we have to announce our coming." And they were still.

The rabbi said, "Go to the door and knock."

It was done, and Quintus came out, saying, "What does this crowd of people want here?"

The rabbi replied that the council had assembled there. Quintus promised to announce them at once, and the rabbi turning to the members of the Sanhedrin, said, "Do you hear? He will announce our presence without delay."

Caiaphas addressed those who were following him: "Ye members of the Sanhedrin, if you have at heart the holy traditions, our honor, the tranquility of the whole land, then consider well this moment. It decides between us and that deceiver. If you are men in whom flows the blood of your fathers, then listen to us. An imperishable monument you will set up for yourselves. Be firm in your resolve."

Then cried the priests, "Our fathers forever; death to the enemy of the nation!"

"Do not rest, then," said Caiaphas, "until he is blotted out of the number of the living!"

And they cried again, "We will not rest, we demand his death, his blood."

Then the soldiers turned to Jesus and said, "Hearest thou that, O king and prophet?"

Then came Pilate out with his attendants upon the balcony of the house; two spearmen on either side advanced to the foot of the steps of the balcony, and stood spear in hand whilst the audience listed. Then Caiaphas stepped forward in front of the crowd, and, bowing low, thus began, "Governor and representative of the great Caesar, health and blessing to thee." Then Caiaphas continued: "We have brought here before thy judgment seat a man of the name of Jesus that thou mayest consent to the execution of the death sentence pronounced against him by the Sanhedrin."

Pilate answered, "Bring him forth," and the soldiers led Jesus, out before Pilate so that he stood on the right hand of the balcony. Pilate having looked upon him asked, "What accusations have you to bring against this man?"

Caiaphas, speaking with some surprise, said, "If he were not a great malefactor we would not have delivered him over to thee, but have dealt with him ourselves according to the direction of our holy law."

"Well, of what evil deeds has he been guilty?" asked Pilate.

Caiaphas answered, "He has in many ways grievously offended against the holy law of Israel."

Pilate answered, "Then take him away and judge him according to your law."

Then said Annas, "He has already been judged by the Sanhedrin and has been declared to be worthy of death."

Then all the priests cried aloud, "For according to our law he has deserved death."

But Caiaphas explained: "It is not lawful for us to execute the sentence of death upon any one; therefore we bring the application for the execution of the sentence to the representative of Caesar."

Then Pilate having looked upon Jesus and upon Caiaphas asked, with indignation, "How can I deliver a man over to death unless I know the crime, and before I have satisfied myself that his crime is worthy of death? What has he done?"

Then said the rabbi, "The sentence of the council upon this man was unanimously pronounced, and grounded upon a careful investigation into his crimes. It seems therefore unnecessary that the illustrious governor should take upon himself the trouble of a second investigation.

"What," said Pilate, hotly, "do you dare to suggest to me, the representative of Caesar, that I should be a blind instrument for the execution of your orders? Be that far from me! I must know what law he has broken, and in what way."

Caiaphas, Annas and the members of the Sanhedrin waxed wroth and spoke warmly among themselves on hearing the words of Pilate. Caiaphas answered and said, "We have a law and by our law he ought to die because he made himself the Son of God," while all the people shouted, "We all have heard the blasphemy from his own lips," and Annas added, "And upon that account we must insist that he suffers the legal punishment."

Then Pilate said scornfully unto them, "On account of such a speech, which at the most is only the outcome of an enthusiastic imagination, a Roman can find no one guilty of death. Who knows also," he added, with a glance at Jesus, "whether this man may not be the son of some god! If you have no other crime to lay to his charge you need not think that I will fulfil your desires."

Caiaphas answered and said, "Not only against our holy law, but also against Caesar himself has this man been guilty of serious offences. We have found him to be an insurgent and deceiver of the people."

Then cried all the priests and Pharisees together tumultuously, "He is an agitator and a rebel."

Pilate answered, "I have heard of one Jesus who was said to go about the country and teach and do extraordinary works, but I have never heard of any sedition stirred up by him. Were anything of that kind to happen I should have heard of it before you, who am appointed for the maintenance of peace in the land, and am perfectly well informed concerning the words and deeds of the Jews. But tell me, when and where has he stirred up any commotion?"

Then Nathanael stood forward and said unto Pilate, "He brings together multitudes by thousands around him and he has quite recently, surrounded by such a crowd, made a solemn entry into Jerusalem itself."

"O I know that," said Pilate contemptuously, "but nothing took place on that occasion to disturb the public peace."

By this time Caiaphas and the priests were in a state of indignation which they did not care to conceal, and Caiaphas asked angrily, "Is it not sedition if he forbid the people to pay tribute to Caesar?"

Pilate asked, "Where have you proof of that?"

"Proof enough," retorted Caiaphas, "for he gives himself out as the Messiah, the king of Israel. Is not that to challenge the imperial authority?"

Pilate replied, sarcastically, "I admire your suddenly awakened zeal for the authority of Caesar."

Then turning to Jesus, who had stood silent during the altercation, he asked him, saying, "Hearest thou what serious accusations these bring against thee? What answerest thou?" Jesus remained silent.

"See," said Caiaphas, eagerly, "He cannot deny it. His silence is an admission of his crime."

Then cried all the multitude, stretching out their hands toward Pilate, "Sentence him then!"

"Patience," said Pilate, "there is time enough for that. I will take him apart for a private hearing."

Pilate, speaking to his attendants, said, "Perhaps when he is no longer confused by the crowd and the fury of his accusers he will answer me." Then, speaking to his servants he said, "Lead him into the court." And turning to Caiaphas and the Sanhedrin, he said, "Go! my guard shall take charge of him, but do you examine the justice or injustice of your complaints, and be careful to investigate whether they do not perhaps come from a polluted source. Then let me know the result of your reflections."

At this Caiaphas turned his back upon Pilate and looked with indignation upon his followers, who showed the liveliest manifestations of disgust. Josue said, "Everything has been well considered and examined already. The law pronounces him worthy of death." The Jews, turning to go, angrily discussed this reverse.

"This is a troublesome delay," said the rabbi.

But Caiaphas encouraged them, saying, "Do not lose heart, victory belongs to the steadfast."

Then was Jesus brought before Pilate's judgment seat, and Pilate said unto him, "Thou hast heard the complaint of the council against thee. Give me an answer thereto. Thou hast, they say, called thyself a Son of God. Whence art thou?" But Jesus made no answer. Then Pilate said unto him with some surprise, "Dost thou not speak even unto me? Knowest thou not that I have power to crucify thee and to release thee?"

Then Jesus turned to him and said, "Thou couldst have no power at all against me except it were given unto thee from above. Therefore he that delivereth me unto thee hath the greater sin."

"Frankly spoken," said Pilate, aside. Then, speaking to Jesus he said, "Art thou the king of the Jews?"

Jesus answered, "Sayest thou this thing of thyself, or only because others have told it to thee?"

Pilate answered, "Am I a Jew? Thine own nation and the chief priests have delivered thee unto me. They accuse thee that thou hast desired to be the king of Israel. What ground is there for this?"

Then answered Jesus and said unto him, "My kingdom is not of this world. If my kingdom were of this world, then would my servants fight, so that I should not be delivered unto the hands of the Jews; but now is my kingdom not from hence."

Then said Pilate, "Art thou a king then?"

Jesus answered, "Thou sayest that I am a king. To this end was I born and for this cause came I into the world, that I might bear witness unto the truth. Everyone that is of the truth heareth my voice."

When Pilate heard this he said, "What is truth?"

Hardly had he asked this question when the servant Quintus entered hastily from the door behind. "Lord, thy servant Claudius is here; he has to bring thee a pressing message from thy wife."

Pilate said, "Let him come in. Lead the man hence for a moment into the hall." The attendants having led Jesus out, Claudius entered. Pilate asked him, "What bringest thou from my dear spouse?"

"My lord," said Claudius, "thy wife greeteth thee and prays thee from her heart, for thine own sake and for hers, that thou wouldst have nothing to do with this just man who has been accused before the judgment seat. She has suffered anguish and terror on his account last night, owing to a fearful dream."

Pilate answered, "Go back and tell her that she need not disturb herself. I will have nothing to do with the proposals of the Jews, but do all that I can to save him." Saluting Pilate, the messenger departed.

Pilate then said to his attendants, "Would that I had nothing to do with this business! What do you think, my friends, of the complaint of the Jewish priests?"

Then said the courtier Mela, "It seems to me that they are only inspired by envy and jealousy. The most passionate hatred appears in their words and countenances."

And the courtier Sylvius added, "The hypocrites pretend that they have the authority of Caesar at heart, whereas the matter concerns only their own authority, which they believe endangered by this famous teacher of the people."

Pilate answered, "I agree with you. I cannot believe that this man entertains any criminal schemes in his mind. There is so much that is noble in his features and in his demeanor. His speech displays so noble a candor and such high natural gifts that he seemed much more to be a very wise man, perhaps only too wise for these gloomy fanatics to be able to bear the light of his countenance. And then the dream which troubled my wife on his account! If he were really of higher origin? No," said Pilate decidedly, arriving at a resolution, "I will not let myself be induced to comply with the wishes of the priests." Then he ordered his servants, saying, "Let the chief priests appear here again, and let the accused be led out again from the judgment hall."

Then came Caiaphas, Annas and the chief priests, and the scribes and rulers of the people once more before Pilate to receive his decision. Then Pilate spoke unto them as follows: "Here you have your prisoner again; he is without guilt." Consternation and fury were displayed on the faces of all the Jews.

Then Annas said, "We have Caesar's word that our law shall be upheld. How can he be without guilt who treads this very law beneath his feet?"

Then cried all the council, saying, "He is worthy of death!"

Caiaphas, who stood before the council, asked, "Is he not punishable by Caesar when he maliciously injures that which Caesar's will has guaranteed us?"

Pilate said, "I have told you already, if he hath done anything against your law, then punish him according to your law, in so far as you are authorized so to do. I cannot pronounce the death sentence upon him, because I find nothing in him which according to the laws upon which I have to act is deserving of death."

Then were the Jews vexed beyond measure and muttered among themselves in hot displeasure, but Caiaphas replied, "If any one proclaims himself as king, is he not a rebel? Does he not deserve the death punishment of high treason?"

"If," said Pilate, "this man has called himself a king it seems to me that so ambiguous a word is not sufficient to condemn him. For it is openly taught among the Romans that every wise man is a king. But you have brought forward no facts to prove that he has usurped kingly authority."

Then said Nathanael, "Is it not a sufficient fact that through him the whole people are stirred up; that he fills the whole of Judea with his teaching, beginning from Galilee, where he first attracted followers to himself, until here in Jerusalem?"

Then asked Pilate in surprise, "Has he come out of Galilee?"

Then cried they all, "Yes, he is a Galilean," and the rabbi added, "His home is in Nazareth, in the jurisdiction of King Herod."

"If that be so, then am I relieved of the jurisdiction. Herod, King of Galilee, has come hither for the feast; he can now judge his own subject. Take him away and bring him unto his own king. He shall be conducted thither by my body guard." Then Pilate with his attendants left the judgment hall.

Caiaphas exclaimed, "Off, then, to Herod! With Herod, who professeth the faith of our fathers, we shall find better protection for our holy law."

Annas said, "And if a thousand hindrances were to oppose themselves, the criminal must meet with the deserved punishment."

Then they cried to Christ, as they went off to the palace of Herod, "One hour sooner or later, what matters it? Thou must come to die, and this very day!"

King Herod stood beside his throne, arrayed in scarlet robes, wearing a golden crown upon his head, and holding a golden scepter in his hand. On either side were his courtiers. He said unto them, "What! have they the famous man from Nazareth? And are they bringing him a prisoner here to me?"

"Yes, my Lord," said Zabulon, "I saw him and recognized him at the first glance."

Then said Herod, "I have for a long time desired to see this man, with whose wondrous works the whole land rings, to whom, as if by magic, people run in crowds. Can he be John, risen from the dead?"

"Oh, no," said Naason, "John worked no miracles; whereas they relate deeds done by this man which in truth are wonderful if they are not exaggerated."

"As I have," said Herod, "so unexpected an opportunity of seeing him, I am impatient to put his magic skill to the proof."

"He will be very willing," said Manasses, "to oblige you in that respect in order to obtain your favor and protection."

Then said Herod, who had seated himself, to Zabulon: "Tell the priesthood they may bring their prisoner in."

"They are probably coming with complaints against this man," said Manasses, "as they are forsaken by all the people."

Herod replied, "Let them do that before Pilate—here I have nothing to do—no judgment to pronounce."

Manasses remarked: "Perhaps they have met with a refusal from the governor and are now siding another way."

Herod replied, "I do not enter into their pious quarrels. I will see him for myself and test his alleged miraculous powers."

Then came into the presence of Herod, Caiaphas, Annas, the rabbi, Nathanael and four priests, bringing Jesus with them led by the soldiers of Herod. Caiaphas bowed before King Herod, saying "Most mighty king," and all the priests cried, "Prosperity and blessing upon thee from the Almighty!"

Then said Caiaphas, "A criminal is brought before thee here from the Sanhedrin, that thou mayest execute on him the judgment of the law."

"The law," said Nathanael, "decrees his death;" and Annas added, "May it please the king to confirm the sentence of the synagogue."

"But," said Herod, "how can I be a judge in a foreign territory? Go to your own governor; he will do justice."

Then said Caiaphas. "Pilate sent him hither, because being a Galilean he is thy subject."

"Then this man belongeth to my jurisdiction? Who is he?"

The priests said, "Jesus of Nazareth."

Caiaphas added, "Pilate himself said, 'Go to King Herod; let him pronounce sentence upon his own subject.'"

"Did Pilate say that? Wonderful!" said Herod. And turning to his courtiers he remarked, "Pilate sends him to me! Allows me to act as judge in his own province!"

A courtier replied, "It seems as if he wished to make approaches to thee again."

Herod replied, "I will accept it as a proof of his friendly feeling."

Then turning to Jesus Herod said, "I have heard very much of thee by common report and have longed to see the man that has created such a sensation in this country."

"He is a deceiver," said the rabbi; "an enemy of the holy law."

"I have heard," said Herod, taking no notice of the interruption, "that thou canst interpret all mysteries and achieve feats which set at defiance the laws of nature. Let us have an example of thy skill and mighty power; then we will honor thee like the people and believe in thee."

"O king," said Zadok, "do not let him lead thee astray, for he is in league with Beelzebub."

"That is all the same to me," said Herod. Then, addressing Jesus, he said, "I had last night a wonderful dream. If thou canst tell me what I have dreamed of I will esteem thee as a first-class reader of hearts."

Herod paused, but Christ remained motionless and silent. "Thou canst not do so much as that," continued Herod, "but perhaps thou understandest how to explain the dream if I tell thee what it was. I dreamt I stood upon the battlements of my palace at Herodium and saw the sun go down. There stood suddenly a man who stretched out his hand and pointed to the setting sun and said, 'See there, there is Hesperia in thy bedchamber.' Hardly had he said this when his form melted into mist. I started and woke up. If thou desirest to be like Joseph when he stood before the King of Egypt interpret to thy king this dream." Christ remained silent, looking sadly at Herod.

"Art thou not experienced in this branch of the business? Well, then, show some of thy famous magic art. Cause it suddenly to become dark in this hall, or raise thyself and depart from us without touching the ground, or convert the roll on which thy death sentence is written into a snake. Thou wilt not, or thou canst not? Any of these things ought to be easy to thee; they relate much more wondrous miracles of thine." Then turning to the courtiers Herod said, "He does not stir. Ah, I see well that what has made him so notorious was only idle tittle-tattle. He knows nothing and can do nothing."

"It is easy," said Naason, "to make believe before the foolish mob; it is another thing to stand before a wise and powerful king."

Then said Manasses to Jesus, "Why should you not display your wisdom here? Why should your power vanish before the eyes of the king, even as a soap bubble?"

Then said Herod scornfully, "There is nothing remarkable about him. He is a conceited fellow whom the applause of the people hath made crazy. Let him go. It is not worth while making so much trouble on his account."

"O, King," said Caiaphas, "do not trust this sly and crafty rogue. Indeed, he only makes himself out to be a fool in order to obtain a milder sentence from thee."

Annas said, "If he be put away, then would the peace of the kingdom also stand in danger, for he has presumed to exalt himself to be king."

"What!" said Herod, "to be a king! To be a king of fools, that is more credible. As such he deserves to receive homage, therefore will I give him as a present a king's mantle, and do formally install him as the king of all fools."

Then cried the priests aloud, "Not this; he has deserved death."

Caiaphas said, "O, King, protector of our holy law, remember thy duty to punish the transgressor as the law ordains."

Then said Herod, "What have you really against him?"

"He hath profaned the Sabbath," said the rabbi.

Nathanael added, "He is a blasphemer."

And all the priests cried, "And as such the law declares him worthy of death."

Then said Ezekiel, "He has also spoken contemptuously of the Temple, which thy father so gloriously rebuilt; he has declared that he would rebuild a more beautiful one in three days."

Then Herod laughed and said, "Now that proves indeed that he is a king of fools."

Then said Jonas, "He has also spoken insultingly of thee. He has presumed to call thee, his lord and king, a fox."

"Then he has attributed to me a quality which he cannot certainly claim himself," replied Herod. "Clothe him—wrapped in this splendid robe he will play his part well before the people."

Then came in a servant bringing a white robe, which he put on the shoulders of Jesus, and after Jesus had been robed, Zabulon said to him, "Now for the first time thou wilt create a real sensation, thou great wonder-worker."

The priests cried, "He must die!"

Herod said, "No, I will not be guilty of the blood of so exalted a king; rather lead him forth before the people in this his proper apparel, that they may admire him to their heart's content."

Then said the first soldier to Jesus, "Come, thou miraculous king, and allow us to accompany thee!"

The second soldier said, "What good luck for me to walk by the side of so illustrious a lord!" And so saying, they led away Jesus, wearing the white robe which Herod had put on him.

Then said Caiaphas, "Thou hast convinced thyself that his alleged great works were nothing but lies and deceit, whereby the people were defrauded by him. Give, then, thy sentence!"

And all the priests cried, "Pronounce the sentence of death upon him, as the law demands!"

Herod replied, "My opinion is, he is a simple fellow and not capable of the crime of which you accuse him. If he has perchance done or spoken anything against the law it is to be attributed to his simplicity."

"O, King," said Caiaphas, "take care that thou dost not err!"

"I fear," said Annas, "thou wilt repent if thou allowest him to escape punishment."

"I fear nothing of the kind," said Herod. "A fool one must treat as a fool. He has already suffered by his follies and will avoid them in the future. With that the trial is at an end."

Then said the rabbi, "Then it is all over with our law, our religion, Moses and the prophets!"

Herod said, "I abide by my decision. I am weary and will not concern myself further about this affair. Pilate may decide according to his official duty. Offer to him duty and friendship from King Herod."

Then went the priests out, sorely dissatisfied with the decision of the king. Then Herod rose from his seat and said, "This time the result has not corresponded to our expectations. I expected to find a great wonder-worker and eloquent orator, and behold, there is only quite an ordinary man with never a word to say for himself."

"Ah," said Manasses, "how lying rumor exaggerates that which, when more closely examined, is shown to be nothing."

"Friends," said Herod, "that is not John. John at least spoke, and spoke with wisdom, and an eloquence which one must esteem, but this one is as dumb as a fish. I am less than ever purposed to put him out of the way, now that I have seen him for myself. Pilate would not have sent him to me if he had been found guilty of any serious crime against the state. To revenge oneself on such a man would be the greatest folly. We have occupied ourselves about this wearisome business long enough. Let us now go and make up for lost time by seeking more agreeable amusement."

CHAPTER VIII

"JESUS OR BARABBAS"

See! what form of woe standeth the Saviour there!
Even Pilate himself's touched with compassion now
Foolish people and blinded,
Have you no hearts to pity him?
No, for seized with madness they cry, "To the cross with him!"
Cry for torture and death upon the holiest.
For Barabbas, the murderer,
Pardon asking, and liberty.
Oh, how otherwise once 'fore the Egyptian folk
Joseph! Around him shouts echoed, and songs of joy
As the Savior of Egypt
He was solemnly shown to them.
But round the world's deliverer rages a nation in wrath,
Blinded, maddened with hate, no man among them will rest
Till the judge all unwilling
Says, "Then take ye and crucify him."

****

Ah, see the king that's crowned in scorn,
What monarch such a crown has worn
Or scepter borne, and he so great?
Ye see him decked with purple shreds,
They laugh and jeer and shake their heads,
Is this the royal robe of state?
Ah! what a man!
Where is the trace of deity?
Ah! what a man—
The sport of the rude hangman he.

Caiaphas and Annas and the chief priests and rulers, and the council and the traders of the temple, and the witnesses accompanied the soldiers, who once more led Jesus to Pilate's house. Then said Caiaphas, "Now Pilate must be challenged more imperiously; and if he does not do according to our will then shall the authority of Caesar extort the sentence from him."

"Shall I now," said Annas, "in my gray old age see the synagogue overthrown? No! with stammering tongue I will cry for the blood and death of this criminal, and then descend to the bosom of my fathers, when I have seen this evil-doer die upon the cross."

"We would sooner," cried the rabbi, speaking with great animation, "be buried in the ruins of the temple than to go back upon our resolution. We shall never leave off until he is dead."

Then proclaimed Caiaphas, "Whosoever goes back on this decision, let him be cast out of the synagogue."

And Annas added, "Let the cross of the fathers fall upon him."

Then said Caiaphas, "Time presses, the day is advancing; now we must employ all the means at our disposal in order to carry out our will before the feast." At this time the Jews and the soldiers leading Jesus stood once more before the house of Pilate.

Pilate, attended by his servants, soon appeared on the balcony.

"We bring the prisoner once more before thee and earnestly desire his death," said Caiaphas.

All the priests cried aloud, "We insist upon it, he must die."

Then said Pilate, "Ye brought me this man as an agitator and see, I have heard your complaints, and I have myself examined him, and have not found anything in him touching those things whereof you accuse him."

Then said Caiaphas angrily, "We abide by our accusation; he is a criminal worthy of death."

And the priests cried, clamorously, "He is an offender against our law and against Caesar."

Then said Pilate, "I have sent him because he is a Galilean to Herod. Have you brought forward your complaints before him?"

"Yes," said Caiaphas, "but Herod would not judge the case because thou art in authority here."

Then said Pilate, "He, too, has found nothing in the man that deserves death, but in order to meet your desire I will have this man scourged and let him go."

But Annas said, "That sufficeth not," and Caiaphas said, "The law prescribes for such a criminal not the punishment of scourging, but the punishment of death."

The priests cried again, "To death with him."

Then Pilate, hearing the clamor of the Jews and seeing how bitter they were against Jesus, said unto them, "Is your hate so deep and bitter unto the man that it cannot be satisfied by the blood from his wounds? You compel me to tell you frankly what I think. Driven by ignoble passion ye persecute him because the people are more devoted to him than they are to you. I have heard enough of your hateful accusations. I will now hear the voice of the people. An innumerable number will now assemble here in order to demand, according to old custom, the release of one prisoner at the Passover festival. Then it will be seen whether your complaint is the outcome of popular sentiment or only of your personal revenge."

Caiaphas, smiling to himself, bowed low before Pilate and said, "The result will show, O governor, that thou thinkest evil of us unjustly."

Then the priests cried, "It is not vengeance, but zeal for the holy law of God which compels us to demand his death."

Pilate said, "You know of the murderer, Barabbas, who lies in chains, and of his evil deeds. Between him and Jesus of Nazareth I will let the people choose. The one whom they ask for, him will I release."

Then cried all with one voice, "Release Barabbas and to the cross with the other."

"You are not the people," said Pilate haughtily, "the people will speak for themselves. Meanwhile I will have this one scourged." Then speaking to his servants, he said, "The soldiers will lead him hence and scourge him according to the Roman law." Then turning to his courtiers, he said, "Whatever he has done amiss will be sufficiently atoned for and perhaps the spectacle of the scourging may soften the blind wrath of his enemies."

When Pilate quitted the balcony and entered his house Caiaphas addressed a stirring speech to the Jews. His opportunity had come.

"Pilate," said Caiaphas, "appeals to the voice of the people. All right; we appeal to it also. Now," said he, turning to the traders and witnesses, "now, true-hearted Israelites, your opportunity has arrived. Go hence into the streets of Jerusalem, summon your friends to come hither, unite them in masses, kindle in them the most glowing hatred against the enemy of Moses. The waverers seek to win by the strength of your words and by promises, but terrify the followers of the Galilean by an overwhelming outcry against them, by insult and mockery, by threats, and if necessary by ill-treatment, so that none of them may dare to let himself be seen here, much less to open his mouth."

Then cried the traders and witnesses together, "We will go hence and soon return again, everyone at the head of an excited mob."

Caiaphas said, "Let us all meet in the street of the Sanhedrin."

The traders bowed, and as they went the priests cried after them, "Hail to you, faithful disciples of Moses."

Then said Caiaphas, "Let us not lose a single moment. Let us go together to the crowds to encourage them, to inflame them."

Annas added, "From all the streets of Jerusalem will we lead the exasperated people before the judgment seat."

The rabbi said complacently, "If Pilate wishes to hear the voice of the people, let him hear it!"

"Let him hear," said Caiaphas, "the unanimous cry of the nation; release Barabbas; the Galilean to the cross!"

Then all the Jews cried aloud, with an exceeding loud voice, "Release Barabbas; the Galilean to the cross!"

Then the soldiers led Jesus away to the Pretorium and took off his robe and tied his hands to a low pillar and scourged him. When they were weary with scourging they said, "He has had enough, he is all running down with blood."

"Thou pitiable king of the Jews," said one of the soldiers as they knelt and mockingly did homage to him, "what kind of a king can this be? He has no scepter in his hand, no crown upon his head. That can be mended. I will at once bring the insignia of the Jewish sovereignty." And then going out he brought a scarlet mantle, a crown of thorns and a reed. They were laid upon a cushion, and together with them were laid iron gloves, so that they might handle the crown of thorns without suffering therefrom.

"Here," cried they, "this is certainly the most lovely attire for a king of the Jews. Is it not true that thou hast never expected such an honor? Come, let us hang this purple robe about thee. But sit down, a king should not stand. Here is a beautiful pointed crown." And a soldier, taking the crown of thorns with the iron gloves, placed it upon the head of Jesus.

"Let us look at you." Then they laughed aloud for joy.

"But," said one, "if it is not to fall off your head then must we set it in firmly. Come, brothers, help me." Then four of the soldiers seized in their hands two staves, and, crossing them over his head, pressed the crown heavily down upon the brow of Jesus. Jesus shuddered in agony.

"Here," cried the soldiers, "is the scepter." And taking the reed they placed it in his hands. "Now nothing more is wanted. What a king!"

Then all knelt before him crying, "Hail to thee, most mighty king of the Jews!" When they were mocking him a servant entered from Pilate, saying that the prisoner mast be brought immediately into the judgment hall.

Then said the soldiers, "Thou comest at the wrong time. Thou hast disturbed us in the middle of our demonstrations of reverence."

Then they said to Jesus, "Stand up, we will lead thee about as a spectacle. There will be rejoicing among the Jewish people when their king appears before them in full splendor!"

Then was Jerusalem in an uproar; the traders and the priests ran everywhere hither and thither, stirring up the people against Jesus. On all sides the crowds were mustered, and directed by the priests to assemble in the streets of the Sanhedrin, and from this to proceed to Pilate's house to demand the release of Barabbas and the crucifixion of Jesus; from four sides the tumultuous mobs came pouring down to the place of assembly. Their hoarse cries of "To the cross with him! To the cross with him!" were heard in the distance before the foremost leaders came in sight. At the head of one mob came Nathanael, fervently exhorting the multitude to demand the death of Jesus.

"Moses, your prophet," said he, "calls upon you. His holy law demands you should avenge it."

And the multitude cried together, "We belong to Moses. We are and remain followers of Moses and of his teaching. We hold fast by our priests and teachers. Away with him who would rise against them." Another multitude poured down from the right into the central thoroughfare. Caiaphas was leading them proudly, exulting in the manifestations of their zeal.

Into the same central place came a third band led by Annas, whose followers shouted aloud, "Ye are our fathers, and we will answer for your honor!"

Annas answered, "Come, children, throw yourselves into the arms of the holy Sanhedrin. It will save you." While the clamorous multitudes from these three quarters were pouring down confusedly into the main street, the shouting of a fourth mob was heard down Pilate's street.

Ezekiel marched at the head of this new company crying, "Shake it off; the yoke of the deceiver!" and they cried in answer, "We will have nothing more to do with him; we follow you!" As the four contingents of the populace collected thus in the open space it could be seen how successfully they had been organized. Each of the four divisions was led by a ruler of the people and had in its ranks a number of the traders of the temple, the witnesses and the priests, whose violent zeal gave movement and direction to the whole crowd. Various cries burst forth from the multitude and each section as it saw the strength of the others exulted and greeted their leaders with shouts of joy. "The whole people applauds you!" cried one part of the multitude.

"We will be free from that false teacher, the Nazarene!" answered another section of the crowd.

Then Caiaphas, Annas, Nathanael and Ezekiel, meeting together, cried with a loud voice, "Your fathers' God will receive you again! You are again to him a holy people!"

The crowd now massed together in the main street cried, "You are our true friends. Long live the great Sanhedrin! Long live our teachers and priests!" and Annas answered, "Death to the Galilean!"

"Up," said Caiaphas, "let us now hasten to Pilate," and Nathanael and Ezekiel added, "Let us demand his death, his blood."

Then all the people answered, "On to Pilate; the Nazarene shall die!"

As they came tripping forward their leaders addressed them from time to time to incite their zeal.

"He hath falsified the law," cried the leaders. "He has contemned Moses and the prophets!" "He hath blasphemed God!"

Then all the people cried again, "To death with the false prophet!"

The section led by Ezekiel shouted, "Death by the cross!" and the other sections took it up, "Pilate must let him be crucified!"

Then said the leaders, "On the cross he shall atone for his crimes!"

"We will not rest," cried the crowd, "until his sentence is pronounced." The whole multitude was now moving rapidly toward the judgment seat of Pilate.

Caiaphas, who lorded it over the whole assemblage with look and gesture, thus addressed them, "Hail to you, children of Israel! You are indeed still true descendants of your father Abraham! Oh, rejoice that you have escaped the nameless destruction which this deceiver would bring upon you and your children!"

"Only," said Annas, "by the untiring efforts of your fathers has this nation escaped the abyss."

Then cried the people, "Long live the council! Death to the Nazarene!" and the priests and Pharisees cried out, "Curse him who does not vote for his death!"

The people responded, "We demand his death!"

Then for some time there was nothing heard but a confused clamor, but the voice of Caiaphas rang out notwithstanding, while the people responded to his appeals. It sounded from afar in this wise: Caiaphas: "Let him be cast out from the heritage of our fathers," and all the people cried, "Let him be cast out."

Caiaphas said, "The governor will give you the choice between this blasphemer and Barabbas. Let us insist upon the release of Barabbas."

Then the people cried, "Let Barabbas go free, and down with the Nazarene."

Then said Annas, "Let the fathers be praised who have heard our wishes."

Then all cried out, "Pilate must consent, the whole nation demands it of him."

Caiaphas walked backward and forward with excited mien, but proud and triumphant step, and said, "Oh, most glorious day of the people of Israel. Children, be steadfast!"

The priests and Pharisees: "This day brings back honor to the synagogue and freedom to the people."

"Now," said Caiaphas, as they approached the house of Pilate, "let us demand the sentence with uproar and threaten him with universal revolt!"

Then cried the whole multitude tumultuously, "We demand the blood of our enemy!"

So loud was the cry, so savage the emphasis, that two servants of Pilate started out of the house and looking down on the turbulent throng cried out, "Uproar! Insurrection!"

And the people answered, "The Nazarene shall die!"

Caiaphas, hastening hither and thither in the crowd to excite them to still further violence, said, "Show courage. Stand out undismayed. A righteous cause defends us."

Then the people called out clamorously; "Pilate—pronounce the sentence of death!"

Pilate's servant from the balcony said, "Silence! be quiet!" but the crowd shouted at him louder than before, "No, we will not be quiet until Pilate consents."

Then said the servant, "Pilate will come out immediately."

Then cried all once more, "We demand the death of the Nazarene."

And Caiaphas, listening to the shouts of the people, said to the priests, "Now let Pilate, as he wished, learn the opinion of the people."

Then came Pilate with his followers out upon the balcony, and with them came Jesus, led by two soldiers, with the crown of thorns upon his head and the scarlet robe about him. The crowd instead of shouting, "Hail, all hail," as before, shouted violently, "Give judgment! Pass sentence upon him!"

Then Pilate spoke, pointing to Jesus, who, with bound hands and the scarlet robe upon his bleeding shoulders, stood between the soldiers, "Behold the man!"

The priests and Pharisees answered, "To the cross with him."

Pilate pleaded, "Cannot even this pitiful sight awake any compassion in your hearts?"

But the multitude answered, "Let him die! To the cross with him!"

Then Pilate said, "Take him and crucify him at your own risk—I will have nothing to do with it, for I find no fault in him."

Then Caiaphas said with a loud voice, "Hear, O governor, the voice of the people. It concurs in our complaint and demands his death."

"Yes," shouted the crowd again, "we demand his death."

Then said Pilate to his soldiers, "Lead him down and let Barabbas be brought out of prison. The jailer must at once deliver him up to the chief lictor."

When Annas heard Pilate's commands he cried, "Let Barabbas live. Pronounce the death sentence on the Nazarene!"

Then the people cried, "To death with the Nazarene!"

Then said Pilate, "I do not understand this, people. Only a few days ago with rejoicing and joyful clamor you accompanied this man through the streets of Jerusalem. Is it possible that the same people this day call for death and destruction upon him? That is indeed contemptible fickleness."

"The good people," said Caiaphas, "have at last learned that they have been deceived by an adventurer who pretended to be the Messiah, the king of Israel!"

"And now," said Nathanael, "the eyes of this people are fully opened, and they see that he cannot help himself—he who promised to bring freedom and blessing to the nation."

"Israel," said Ezekiel, "will recognize no Messiah who allows himself to be taken and bound and treated with scorn."

"Let him die, the false Messiah, the deceiver," cried the crowd.

Then Pilate spoke unto the people and said: "Men of Judea, it is customary that I liberate to you a prisoner at the feast. Look upon these two. One with mild countenance and dignified demeanor, the ideal of a wise teacher, whom you have long honored as such, convicted of no single evil deed and already humiliated by the severest chastisement. The other, a vicious, savage man, convicted of robbery and murder, a horrible image of a perfect scoundrel. I appeal to your reason, to your human feelings—choose! Which will ye that I shall release unto you, Barabbas or Jesus, who is called the Christ?"

Then the priests and people cried out together, "Let Barabbas go free."

"Will ye not that I release unto you the king of the Jews?" asked Pilate.

Then the priests and people cried, "Away with him, release unto us, Barabbas."

Then said Caiaphas, "Thou hast promised to release him whom the people demand."

Pilate answered shortly to Caiaphas, "I am accustomed to keep my promise without needing a reminder." Then said he to the people, "What shall I do with the king of the Jews?"

And the priests and the people cried, "Crucify him!"

"What," said Pilate, "shall I crucify your king?"

And the people cried, "We have no king but Caesar."

Pilate said, "I cannot condemn this man, for I find no fault in him. He has been sufficiently chastised; I will let him go free."

Then said the priests, "If thou let him go free thou art no friend of Caesar's."

Caiaphas added, "He has proclaimed himself king"; and the priests said, "Who proclaims himself king is a rebel against Caesar."

And Nathanael said, "And is this rebel still to remain unpunished, still to scatter abroad the seed of revolt?"

Then cried the people, "It is the duty of the governor to put him out of the way."

Caiaphas seeing that Pilate answered not, pressed more vehemently upon him, saying, "We have done our duty as subjects of Caesar and delivered this rebel to thee. If thou payest no attention to our accusation and the desire of the people, then are we free from guilt. Thou alone, O Governor, art responsible to Caesar for the consequences."

And Annas said, "If on account of this man universal disorder and revolt ensues, then we know who must bear this guilt, and," he added significantly, "Caesar shall know it also."

Then cried the people again, "The matter must be brought before Caesar."

Then Ezekiel said to Pilate, "They will be astonished when they hear at Rome that Caesar's viceroy has taken under his protection a traitor whose death the whole people desired."

And the crowd cried, "Thou must execute him, or otherwise there would be no peace in the land."

Then said Pilate, "Why, what evil hath he done? I cannot, I dare not, condemn the innocent to death."

Then said Caiaphas, "Permit me to ask one question. Why shouldst thou judge this man so carefully when quite recently thou hast allowed thy soldiers to massacre hundreds without judgment or sentence, merely on account of some rebellious outcries?"

As Pilate heard the question of Caiaphas he was dismayed, and the crowd shouted: "Thou canst not show favor to this man; if thou wilt be a faithful servant to Caesar."

Then Pilate's resolution forsook him, and turning to his servants he said, "Bring water."

Caiaphas said unto him, "The people will not go away from this place until thou hast pronounced sentence of death upon the enemy of Caesar."

"Yes," cried the multitude, "we will not go from this place until sentence is pronounced."

Then said Pilate sorrowfully, "Your violence compels me to yield to your desire. Take him hence and crucify him. But see," said he as he washed his hands in the basin which had been brought at his command. "I wash my hands; I am innocent of the blood of this just man. See ye to it."

Then arose from the excited multitude a great and awful cry, in which priests and people joined, speaking as with one voice, "We take it upon ourselves! His blood be upon us and upon our children!"

Then said Pilate, "Let Barabbas be set free at the demand of the people. Lead him outside the city gate and let him never tread this ground again." The soldiers then led Barabbas away.

The priests and people cried: "Now hast thou justly judged."

Pilate said unto them, "I have given way to your violent demands in order to avoid a great evil. But in the blood-guiltiness I will have no share. Let it fall upon you and your children as you have so loudly cried."

Then again the priests and people cried, "It is good; let it fall upon us and upon our children."

Annas said, "We and our children will bless this day and with thankful joy cry, 'Health and wealth to the governor!'"

"Long live our governor," cried the crowd. "Long live Pontius Pilate!"

Then said Pilate, "Bring hither the two murderers who are kept in gaol. Let the chief lictor give them over without delay to the guard. They have deserved death much more than the accused."

But the priests and people cried, "He has deserved death more than any."

Pilate said, "The sentence of death must be written out and will be read publicly before all the people."

The scribe began to write, and as he wrote, from the street were heard the voices of the soldiers who were bringing the thieves, driving them forward: "Will you not move on, you wretches? Have you not long ago deserved your fate? Thrust them on, these outcasts of mankind." When the thieves driven by the soldiers came to the foot of the balcony they were halted on the other side of the steps to that where Jesus stood.

Then said the rabbi, pointing to the thieves, "That is worthy company for the false Messiah on his last journey."

Pilate said to the thieves, "Of you and your misdeeds the earth shall today be free. You shall die upon the cross. Let the sentence of death be now read."

Then the scribe stood forward and read thus: "I, Pontius Pilate, viceroy in Judea of the mighty Caesar Claudius Tiberius, pronounce at the desire of the high priests and the Sanhedrin and the people of the Jews, the sentence of death upon a certain Jesus of Nazareth, who is accused of having stirred up the people to revolt, of having forbidden to pay tribute to Caesar, and of having proclaimed himself king of the Jews. The same shall be crucified outside the city between two malefactors who have been likewise condemned to death for many robberies and murders, and be brought from life to death. Given at Jerusalem on the eve of the Passover."

When the scribe had read the sentence Pilate broke a staff, flung it among the people, saying in tones of great bitterness, "Now take him hence and crucify him!" and went rapidly into the house, leaving Jesus in the hands of the Jews.

"Triumph!" cried Caiaphas in wild exultation. "The victory is ours! The enemy of the synagogue is destroyed!"

The priests and people shouted, "Away with him to Golgotha! Long live the synagogue! Long live the nation!"

Then said Annas, "Hasten, that we may come home in time to eat the Passover."

The priests and Pharisees said, "We will keep this Passover with joy, as did our fathers in Egypt."

"Now," said Caiaphas, "let our triumphal procession go through the midst of Jerusalem."

"Where," asked the rabbi, "are his disciples? They are invited to cry Hosanna!"

Then rushed the multitude away, crying, "Up and away off to Golgotha! Come and see him perish on the cross! O delightful day, the enemy of Moses is overthrown! Ha! now he has his reward! So be it done to everyone who despises the law! He deserves the death on the cross! O happy Passover! Now joy will return to Israel! There is an end of the Galilean!" And so crying, with wild and savage clamor, they swept back to the street of the Sanhedrin.

[Transcriber's note: A line seems to be missing from the book at this point. All that appears is a blank line followed by the single word:] "me?"

CHAPTER IX

THE CRUCIFIXION

> Ye pious souls rise up and go,
> With grateful penitence aglow
> With me to Golgotha, and see
> What shall be done your souls to free
> See how the Mediator dies
> The atoning death of sacrifice.
>
> O, who can know the love that lives
> In this heart now laid bare,
> That kindness back for hatred gives
> And saves us from despair?
> Offer this love of His
> Your heart's best impulses,
> His cross before,
> For evermore.

Thus they took Jesus and led him away, and a great multitude followed him. And when Jesus, bearing the cross, with the thieves also bearing their cross, was entering the street of Annas, Mary, the mother of Jesus, with Mary Magdalene and John and Joseph of Arimathea, came down the street by Pilate's house.

And Mary said to John, "O beloved disciple, how will it have gone with Jesus since thou didst last see him in the house of Caiaphas?"

Then answered John, "If the priests could do as they wish, then sure enough he would be already among the dead. But they could not carry out the sentence without permission of the governor. But Pilate, I hope, will not condemn him, as he has never done anything bad, but only what is good."

Then prayed Mary Magdalene, "O Almighty God, incline the ruler's heart to justice, that he may protect the innocent against the wiles of the wicked."

Then said Mary, the mother of Jesus, "Whither shall we go, O friends, oh, whither, that I may but once more see my beloved son? I must see him, but where can I find him? Perhaps, O perhaps, he lies buried in the deepest dungeon."

Mary Magdalene said, "Alas! the most loving of teachers in prison!"

Joseph answered, "There is one to be seen from whom we can inquire."

John said, "The best thing will be to go to Nicodemus; he surely knows what is happening to our dear Master."

"Yes, let us go," said Mary. "Every moment increases my grief in this uncertainty about the fate of my son."

"Be strong in faith, dear mother," said John. "Whatever happens it is God's will." Suddenly a horrible noise of confused voices and tramping feet was heard in the distance. From the tumult could be heard the words: "On, on with him!" Mary started and they all stood listening while the noise came nearer and nearer.

"What terrible noise is that?" said Joseph. Then stood they all still listening to hear what it might signify.

Salome said, "As if of a thousand voices. What can it be?"

As they listened the procession to Golgotha was already half way down the street of Annas. In front marched the centurion holding in one hand the staff of authority, followed by Jesus, staggering painfully under the burden of his cross. Around Jesus stood four executioners who brutally goaded him forward. Behind Jesus came the thieves, each bearing his own cross. Behind them came soldiers carrying spears, in the midst of whom on a white horse rode a horseman carrying the Roman banner on which were the letters S. P. Q. R. By the side of the soldiery walked Annas and Caiaphas followed by all the council of the Sanhedrin. All around crowded a numerous multitude, whose shouts were heard almost without intermission. "Let him die!" they cried, "and all who hold with him." Jesus, who had already fallen under the cross, walked slowly and with difficulty.

One of the executioners said unto him, "Is the burden already too heavy?" and the people shouted, "Drive him with violence, that we may get to Golgotha."

The second executioner cried, "Take care, or he will be down."

The progress was so slow that not even the head of the procession could be seen from where the two Marys and John were standing, wondering what the noise might mean.

Joseph said, "What shall we do? In this commotion we cannot venture into the city."

But Mary said, "What may this noise signify? Surely it does not concern my son."

As the noise waxed ever louder, Joseph said, "It seems as if an insurrection had broken out."

Then said John, "We had better stop here till the storm passes over."

While they stood waiting and wondering Simon of Cyrene came hastily into the street that lay between those of Pilate and Annas. He carried a basket, and looking anxiously around him, said, "I must hasten in order to get into the city. The eve of the feast is coming, and I have only a short time left in which to make my purchases and get everything ready, so that I may get home in time." Hardly had he said this than he heard the sound of a great outcry, and amidst which he could only distinguish the words, "Let him not rest! Urge him on with blows!"

Said Simon, "I hear a tumult—an outcry of a crowd—what has happened in the city? I will keep quiet a little—perhaps my ears have deceived me." Jesus had fallen faint and had staggered against the house of Ahasverus and was there endeavoring to support himself.

The third executioner said to him roughly, "It is no use thy fainting. Thou must keep on to Golgotha."

Then Ahasverus came out of his house and said, "Be off from my house; here is no place for resting." Simon, who was listening without being able to see the cause of the commotion, said, "The noise waxes louder. I must hasten to see what it is. What comes there? Ah, I cannot get in here. I will wait and see what happens."

Then, as the procession turned the corner of Annas' street, Joseph of Arimathea, listening, said, "I think the crowd is coming out of the city gates," and John, seeing the cross said, "It appears that someone is being led out to Golgotha for execution."

Mary, the mother of Jesus, saw him and cried out with a piercing wail, "It is he. Oh God! it is my son."

Jesus meanwhile staggered under the cross, but was forced forward by the executioners grumbling as they did so, "He will drop on the road."

The centurion, seeing that Jesus from sheer exhaustion had again fallen, reached him a bottle, saying, "Here, strengthen thyself." Jesus took it, but did not drink of it.

Mary cried, weeping, "Ah, there, I see him led to death even as a malefactor!"

Then said John, as he tenderly supported her, "Mother, it is the hour of which he has told us before. Such is the will of the Father."

Then said the centurion to Jesus, "Wilt thou not drink? Then you must go on!"

Then one of the executioners shook him, saying, "Rouse thyself, lazy king of the Jews!"

Another of the executioners said, "Forward! Pull thyself together!" The third said, "Do not act thus weakly; we must get on."

Then Mary cried as she looked on the scene, "Oh where is any sorrow like unto my sorrow?"

The third executioner, seeing that all the efforts to compel Jesus to move forward had failed, said, "He is too much exhausted; someone must help him, otherwise—"

Then the rabbi, seeing Simon of Cyrene, pointed him out, saying, "Here, this stranger—"

The Pharisees said, "Just seize him!"

Then said the centurion, "Come hither, thou hast broad shoulders that can carry something."

Simon, protesting, said, "I must—"

"Truly you must," said one of the executioners, "otherwise there will be blows."

Simon began again, "I do not know," but the centurion interrupted him, saying, "You will find out soon enough—do not refuse."

"Flog him if he refuses to go!" said the Pharisee.

Simon struggled crying, "Indeed I am innocent; I have committed no crime."

"Silence!" said the centurion.

Simon replied, "Only not by force like this," and then beholding Christ he said, "What is this I see? This is the holy man from Nazareth."

"Place thy shoulders here," said an executioner.

Then said Simon, "For the love of thee I will carry it. O, could I thereby make myself useful to thee."

Christ, who stood exhausted on one side, looked upon Simon and said, "God's blessing be upon thee and thine!"

"Now, forward," said the centurion; "follow thou with the beam of the cross!"

The first priest advancing, said, "Thou canst come quickly enough now."

The third executioner, seeing that Jesus still stood unable to move, seized him by the neck and shook him saying, "See with what consideration we treat thee; even the cross has been taken from thee."

"Dost thou need anything else?" said another of the men.

"Let him be," said the centurion. "We will now halt a little that he may recover before we ascend the hill."

While the procession halted Veronica and the women of Jerusalem approached. Caiaphas meanwhile, chafing with vexation at the delay, exclaimed, "What! Still another stoppage! When shall we come to Calvary?"

Veronica, coming up to Christ, kneeled before him, and offering him her handkerchief, said, "O Lord, how is thy face covered with blood and sweat. Wilt thou not wipe it off?"

Jesus took the handkerchief and wiped his face and gave it back to her, saying, "Compassionate soul, the Father will reward thee for this."

Then spoke the women of Jerusalem, who drew near to the Lord with their little ones, "Thou good teacher; never to be forgotten benefactor; noblest friend of men, thus art thou rewarded. How we pity thee!" Then they wept.

Christ looking upon them in their tears said: "Daughters of Jerusalem, weep not for me, but for yourselves and your children. For behold the days are coming in which they shall say 'Blessed are the barren and the wombs that never bare, and the paps that never gave suck.' Then shall they call to the mountains, fall on us and to the hills, cover us. For if they do these things in the green tree, what will be done in the dry?"

The women answered, "Alas, how will it be in the future for us and our children?"

By this time the patience of the centurion was exhausted, and he cried out, "Clear out now, these womenfolk."

The third executioner, pushing them roughly away, said, "What use are your women's tears? Back!" While the other executioners cried as they pushed Jesus forward, "On with thee to the hill of death!"

The crowd took up the cry and said, "Quick; forward to Calvary!"

"Are we really going forward again?" said the rabbi, and Nathanael said, shrugging his shoulders, "The centurion is far too mild."

"Do not spare him so much," said a priest.

The long procession was once more in motion when there appeared a servant from Pilate. The man cried, "Halt!" and the procession stopped. "By command of the governor the centurion must appear before him as quickly as possible and receive further orders."

Caiaphas exclaimed, "What does this mean? What new orders are required? The death sentence is pronounced and must be carried out without delay."

Then said the centurion bluntly, "No, this will not happen until I have received the further orders of my lord." Then turning to the soldiers he said, "Keep watch meanwhile and go with the condemned to Golgotha. Then dismiss this man (Simon) and await my arrival." The centurion then went with the servant to Pilate and the procession set forth again.

The people cried wildly, "Up to Golgotha, to the cross with him. Hail to Israel. The enemy is vanquished. We are free. Long live the Sanhedrin."

Jesus looked upon his mother as the procession passed the corner of Annas' street, but spoke not.

Then said John, when the dolorous procession had passed, "Mother, shall we not go back to Bethany? Thou wilt not be able to bear the sight?"

But Mary answered, "How can a mother leave her child in the last and bitterest need?"

Cleophas objected, "But evil might befall thee, if they recognized thee as his mother."

Mary replied, "I will suffer with him, bear scorn and shame with him; die with him."

"Only," said John, "if the strength of thy body does not give way."

"Fear not," said Mary. "I have asked strength of God and he has heard me. Let us go after them."

All answered, "Best of mothers, we follow thee," and they slowly followed the procession to Calvary.

And when they reached Golgotha, which is by interpretation the place of a skull, they crucified him there. But first they hanged the two thieves on the crosses, the one on the left, the other on the right. Their arms were tied over the cross at the wrists, and their feet were tied with cord to the beam. But Jesus was nailed to the central cross while it yet lay with the head slightly raised upon the ground. One nail was driven through the palms of each hand, and one through the two feet, which were placed the one above the other. Jesus lay silent without moving. On his head was the crown of thorns, from which a little blood trickled over his brow. His hands and his feet bled a little, but the rest of his body was pale and colorless, a light cloth only being cast around his loins.

The centurion who had returned from Pilate, stood on the right of the cross giving orders. The lictor, mounted on a white horse, stood near the soldiers, who held on high the Roman standard with the letters S. P. Q. R. Caiaphas, Annas and all the members of the Sanhedrin stood on the left exulting. A great crowd of sightseers thronged the place. Among them, coming from behind the centurion, were the holy women from Bethany, with Mary, the mother of Jesus, and John, and Joseph of Arimathea and Nicodemus.

Then said the executioners to the centurion, "We have finished with these," pointing to the thieves, "Now must the king of Jews be exalted upon his throne."

Which, hearing, the priests cried angrily, "Not king! Deceiver, traitor!"

The centurion, who held in his hand a scroll or escutcheon, said, "First, by command of the governor, this writing must be fastened to the cross. Faustus," he added, turning to one of the hangmen named Faustus, "make fast this title over the cross." Faustus took the scroll from the centurion, and going to the cross, nailed it with one hammer stroke over the head of Jesus, saying, "Ah, an escutcheon displayed; this is right royal!" When this was done according to the command of the governor, the centurion said to the executioners, "Now, up with the cross! Not carelessly, but lay hold firmly." Then two hangmen, taking the cross by the arms, lifted it up so that its foot fell into the hole prepared for it. But as the cross bearing the body of Jesus was heavy, the third hangman placed his back under it near to the feet of Jesus, saying, "Come, now, all together," and so helping raised it on high. The fourth then filled in the hole at the foot saying when he finished, "All right, the cross stands firm."

Then said the centurion, addressing the chief priests, "The execution is accomplished."

"Quite admirably so," said Caiaphas with a radiant face. "Thanks and applause from us all!" "Yea, thanks, and applause from us all," echoed the Pharisees, looking up at the cross.

Caiaphas then declared, "This shall be a feast day forever."

And the Pharisees said, "Yes, for all time to come it shall be kept every year with grateful jubilation."

"And now," said the aged Annas, "now gladly will I go down to my fathers since I have lived to have the joy of seeing this wretch on the cross." And as he gazed long as if exultingly drinking in the pleasure of satisfied vengeance, he saw for the first time the writing on the cross, but his old eyes could not decipher the words. Turning to Caiaphas he said, "The superscription seems to be very short." Then the Jews drew nearer to see what was written. The hangmen seated themselves on the ground at the foot of the cross and looked up at Jesus.

Then the rabbi, reading the words written by Pilate exclaimed, "That is an insult, an outrage upon the people and the Sanhedrin!"

Caiaphas, hearing him, asked, "What is written?"

Annas, who had also looked at the inscription, said, "The rabbi is right. The Sanhedrin cannot allow this to pass."

Then said the rabbi, "It is written, 'Jesus of Nazareth, king of the Jews!'"

Caiaphas as if incredulous, approached the cross and reading it himself, started back with indignation. "Verily," he cried, "that is an affront upon the honor of our nation."

"Down with it at once," cried the priest.

But Caiaphas said, "We dare not touch it ourselves, but do you two," addressing the rabbi and Saras, "hasten at once to the governor to demand from him, in the name of the Sanhedrin and the assembled people that the superscription shall be altered. Say to him, 'Write not the king of the Jews, but that he said, I am king of the Jews?'"

"We are off at once," said the rabbi and Saras.

"Stay," said Caiaphas, "also request from the governor that he may order the bones of the crucified to be broken and their bodies taken down from the cross before the eve of the Passover."

When the rabbi and Saras departed on their mission, the hangmen, who had been sitting at the foot of the cross, bethought themselves, and the first, who was named Agrippa, standing up, said, "Now, comrades, let us divide our share." Taking the mantle of Jesus, they seized each one corner, and then pulling all together, rent it into four parts. The coat remained. Agrippa held it up, "The mantle has made just four pieces; shall we rip up the coat also? See, it is without seam."

"No," said Faustus, who had fastened the superscription over the head of Jesus, "it would be better to cast lots for it."

"Look," said Agrippa, as he went to the foot of the cross and took up the basket, "see, here are dice." Then the four hangmen, standing at the feet of Jesus threw the dice, Agrippa threw them first, saying, "I will try my luck first. Alas, that is too little," he added, as he counted up the result of his throw, "I have lost."

Catiline, the third hangman, as he rattled the dice in his hand, looked up at Jesus and said, "Hi! you up there, if you can still work miracles on the cross, give me good luck." The others shrugged their shoulders and said, "What does he care about us?" Catiline's throw was not high.

Then Nero said, "I ought to have had better luck," and throwing the dice he counted fifteen. "Nearly enough; now, Faustus, it is your turn."

Faustus threw the dice, saying, "I ought to get it." They all bent over to see the result.

"Eighteen!" cried Catiline; "that is the best yet."

Then said Agrippa, "Take it," handing him the mantle, "it is thine; take it away."

And Nero consoled himself by saying, "You are not to be envied."

Faustus gathered up the coat, and folding it up put it away.

By this time the rabbi and Saras returned from Pilate, and coming back to Caiaphas they said, "Our mission was in vain. The governor would not listen to us."

Caiaphas indignantly asked, while the priests and Pharisees crowded around, "Did he give you no answer at all?"

"This only," said the rabbi. "What I have written I have written."

"Intolerable," said Annas.

Caiaphas also was much perturbed. But collecting himself he asked, "What did he order about the breaking of the bones?"

"About this matter he said he would give his orders to the centurion," answered the rabbi.

Then seeing that no more could be done, the Jews began to revile Jesus, going up to the cross and wagging their heads and scoffing at him. Josue, the priest, went up first and said, "So then it remains written, king of the Jews. Behold, if thou art king of Israel, come down now from the cross, that we may see and believe." And all the Jews laughed together.

Then said Eliezer, "Thou that destroyest the temple and buildest it again in three days, save thyself!"

And Caiaphas said, "Ha! thou that savest others, thyself thou canst not save."

"Come down," cried one of the witnesses, "Art thou not the Son of God?"

And Annas said, "He trusted in God; let him deliver him now if he will have him."

Then cried the hangmen, "What! Don't you hear? Show thy power, mighty king of the Jews," and so the sport went on.

Then Jesus, who all this time had hung motionless and silent, raised slowly and with pain, his head, which had been bowed down, and said, "Father, forgive them, they know not what they do!"

Hearing Jesus speak, the thief who was crucified on his left said unto him, "Hearest thou? If thou be Christ save thyself and us."

But the other thief who was crucified on the right, answered and said, "Dost thou not fear God, seeing that thou art in the same condemnation? And we indeed justly; for we receive the due reward of our deeds; but this man hath done nothing amiss." Then turning to Jesus he said, "Lord remember me when thou comest into thy kingdom?"

Then Jesus looked upon him and said, "Verily, I say unto thee, today shalt thou be with me in Paradise."

"Listen to that," said Caiaphas scornfully, "he speaks as if he had power over the gates of Paradise."

"What," said the rabbi. "Have not his pride and presumption deserted him even as he hangs helpless on the cross?" And they were wroth with Jesus.

During all this time Mary, the mother of Jesus, and John had been slowly approaching the cross, and now they stood immediately below Jesus, Mary on the right, John on the left. Then Jesus beholding them, said to Mary, "Mother, behold thy son." And slowly and with difficulty turning his head to see John, Jesus added, "Son, behold thy mother."

Then Mary cried in ecstacy of love and adoration, "Even in dying thou carest still for thy mother."

And John tenderly supporting Mary, but looking above to Jesus, exclaimed, "Thy last request is sacred to me."

And then to Mary he said, "Thou my mother, I thy son."

Then Jesus in a hollow voice, cried hoarsely, "I thirst."

The centurion hearing him said, "He thirsts and calls for drink."

"Then," said Faustus, "I will reach him some at once." Then taking the reed with the sponge, he filled it with vinegar and passed it to the centurion, who, taking a small phial from his dress, poured hyssop on the sponge. Faustus then reached the sponge up to the lips of Jesus. But Jesus turned away his head and would not drink. "Here, drink," said Faustus. "What, wilt thou not?" and seeing that Jesus would not touch the sponge he took it away.

Then Jesus cried in agony, "Eli, Eli, lama sabachthani!"

But those hearing him did not understand, but imagined he cried for Elias.

"Hark!" said they. "He cried for Elias."

Then Caiaphas laughed and said, "Let be; let us see whether Elias will come to save him."

Then Jesus raising his head with a great effort to heaven, and breathing heavily cried with a loud voice and said, "It is finished.

Father, into thy hands I commend my spirit!" And as Jesus spoke these words his head fell forward on his breast and he gave up the ghost. Then suddenly the earth rocked and shook violently—thunder pealed—fierce lightnings flashed—darkness fell like a pall over the scene—the people stood trembling with fear.

The priests and the people cried out in terror, saying: "What a dreadful earthquake! Do you hear the crash of falling rocks? Woe, woe be to us!"

But the centurion said, "Certainly, this was a righteous man."

Another soldier replied, "God himself bears witness by these convulsions of nature."

The centurion said, "Oh, his patience in the worst agony, his noble calm, this last loud cry to heaven at the moment before death, all betoken his divine origin. Verily, he is a Son of God!"

"Come neighbors," said Oziel, "I will remain no longer in this terrible place."

"Yes," cried Helen, "let us go home and may God have mercy on us."

And others smiting their breasts cried, "Almighty God, we have sinned! Forgive us."

And so it came to pass that no one remained round the cross but the holy women and John, and the friends of Jesus with the hangmen.

The chief priests and the rulers still stood together marveling near the cross of the repentant thief, when suddenly a temple servant came rushing into their midst, breathless with haste.

"High priests and assembled council!" he exclaimed, "a fearful thing has occurred in the holy place. I tremble in every limb."

"What is it?" cried Caiaphas in alarm. "Not the temple?"

"Has it fallen?" said Annas.

"No," said the servant, "not that, but the veil of the temple has been rent in twain from the top to the bottom. I hastened hither with staggering feet, and feared the whole world was bursting asunder with the shock!"

"Dreadful!" exclaimed the priests and Pharisees, throwing up their hands.

But Caiaphas said, "It is that wretch who has done this by his magic arts. What a blessing it is that he is out of the world! Otherwise he would bring all the elements into disorder."

Then all the priests and Pharisees raised up their voices and cried, shaking their fists against Jesus, "Cursed be the ally of Beelzebub!"

"Now," said Caiaphas, "let us hurry home and see what has happened; then we will come back at once. For I cannot rest until I have seen this fellow's bones broken and the corpse flung into the grave of the transgressors."

When Caiaphas and Annas and all the rulers of the Jews had departed, Nicodemus said to Joseph of Arimathea, having overheard the parting word-of Caiaphas, "Shall the holy body of the Son of God be delivered over to such dishonor as to be flung into the grave of the evil-doers?"

"Listen, friends," said Joseph, "what I have decided to do. I will go straightway to Pilate, and will implore him to give me the body of Jesus. He can hardly refuse me this favor."

"Do so, by all means," said Nicodemus. "Hasten hither, and I will bring the spices for him." They having departed, the holy women tremblingly drew round the cross.

"Fear not, good women," said the centurion, "no harm shall happen to you."

Then Mary Magdalene clasped the cross with both her arms, pressed it to her breast and cried through her tears as she looked up at the silent and lifeless form above, "O dearest Master, my heart hangs with thee on the cross!"

Then entered a servant of Pilate, and addressing the centurion, said unto him, "This is the command of my lord: Break the legs of the crucified and take down their bodies. Everything must be over before the eve of the Passover begins."

The centurion said: "It shall be done at once. Men, first break the legs of these two."

Catiline said, "Come, let us put this business through without more delay." Then all the hangmen took ladders and placed them against the crosses of the thieves. Catiline, seizing a strong club, then mounted the ladder against the cross on the right hand.

"Strike," said Faustus, "so as to kill him." Then Catiline smote the penitent thief heavily over each of the thighs and then across the shoulder bone. As the blow fell the man's head fell forward and he gave up the ghost.

"There," said Catiline, "he wakes no more."

In like manner did Nero to the thief on the left hand, saying, "I will hasten the other out of the world."

When the blows were falling upon the body of the thief, Mary, the mother of Jesus, who had watched with terror the blows of the hangman, cried out, shuddering, "O my Son, they will surely not deal so cruelly with thy holy body!"

Nero called out to the thief, "Movest thou no more? No, thou hast had enough. I have given thee thy wages." Then coming down from the ladder they made ready to break the legs of Jesus.

But as the hangman approached the foot of the cross with the ladder and the club, Mary Magdalene sprang before him, and thrusting him back with her slender arm, cried piteously, "Oh, spare him, spare him!"

Then Catiline looking up at Jesus said, "Behold, he is already dead. There is no need therefore to break his legs."

"But," said Faustus, "in order to make sure, I will pierce his heart with a spear." Then grasping a lance he thrust it into the right side of Jesus, and forthwith there spurted out blood and water. John, who was looking up at the holy women, shuddered as the spear entered the side of Jesus.

Mary Magdalene turning to Mary said, "Oh, mother, that thrust hast pierced thy own heart also."

Then said the centurion, "Now, take down the bodies from the cross."

"Where," said one of the hangmen, "shall we put them?"

The centurion replied, "As ordered, into the grave of the malefactor."

Then said Mary, with a terrible sob: "What a word; it pierces my heart anew."

"Ladders here," said the hangmen, "we shall soon have them down." Then the hangmen unfastened the cords which bound the thieves to their crosses, and mounting the ladder received their bodies in their arms and bore them away.

While they were busy Mary Magdalene went out to the centurion and said to him: "May we not even pay the last honors to our friend?"

"Alas," said the centurion, "it is not within my power to permit this."

Then came back Caiaphas and Annas and all the rulers of the Sanhedrin from the temple to Golgotha. Caiaphas, speaking as they approached, said, "It will be all the more delightful to see the body of this evil-doer cast into the pit of shame, because we have witnessed the destruction he has brought to pass within the temple."

Annas answered, "What joy it would be if my eyes could see him torn limb from limb by wild beasts."

"Ha," said Caiaphas, as they saw the hangman bearing off the bodies of the thieves, "they are already being taken down. Now we shall soon see our ardent desires fulfilled."

Hardly had Caiaphas and the priests approached the cross when from the other side there came Joseph of Arimathea and with him a servant of Pilate. The servant said to the centurion, "The governor has sent me to inquire of thee whether it can really be true that Jesus of Nazareth is already dead as this man has informed me."

"It is so, indeed," replied the centurion, pointing to the cross. "Look for yourself. Besides, for a complete certainty, his heart has been thrust through with a lance."

Then said the servant, "I have orders to inform you that the body is to be delivered over to this man as a gift from Pilate." And having said this he departed.

"Oh, blessed tidings!" cried the holy women still gathered together around the foot of the cross.

But the Jews hearing the message, waxed furious and the rabbi, speaking of Jesus, said to the other priests and rulers, "The traitor of the synagogue, he has fooled us again."

"And spoiled our triumph," said Annas.

But Caiaphas would not submit and said haughtily, "We shall not tolerate it that his body be laid anywhere else than in the grave of the transgressors."

The centurion replied, "As the body is given to this man, it is obvious that he can bury it where and how he will. There is no disputing that."

Then he said to the soldiers and executioners, "Men, our work is done. We will return."

Then the hangmen gathered up their basket and their cord, their dice and the fragments of Christ's mantle and departed. With them went the centurion and his band, leaving Caiaphas and the Jews face to face with the holy women and their friends at the foot of the cross. The Jews were exceedingly wroth and raged amongst themselves at the centurion.

Annas cried out to Joseph of Arimathea, "Dost thou still persist in thy headstrong obstinacy? Art thou not ashamed to do honor to the very corpse of an executed malefactor?"

Joseph replied, "I indeed honor this noblest of men, the teacher sent from God, whom being innocent you have murdered."

And Nicodemus added, "Envy and pride were the motives of his condemnation. The judge himself was forced to bear witness to his innocence, and swore he would have no part in his death."

Then said Caiaphas furiously, "The curse of our law will destroy you, ye enemies of our fathers."

The rabbi said, "Do not excite thyself about them, O, high priest; they are smitten with blindness."

But Caiaphas, refusing to be silenced, cried, "Cursed are ye by the holy council. Deprived of all your honors, never more shall ye dare to take your seats in our midst."

"Neither do we desire to do so," said Nicodemus.

Then said Annas, "As the body is now in the hands of his friends, we must be on our guard, for this deceiver, while he was yet alive said that in three days he would rise again."

The rabbi said, "They could easily practice a new deception on the people and make fresh trouble for us. His disciples might take his body away secretly and then give out that he had risen from the dead."

"In that case," said Caiaphas, "the last error would be worse than the first. Let us therefore go at once to Pilate and ask him for a guard of soldiers to keep watch over the grave until the third day."

"A prudent thought," cried Annas, and the rabbi added, "Thus their schemes will be foiled." Then they departed to go to Pilate.

His enemies having left his friends alone around the cross, Nicodemus and Joseph set about taking down the body of Jesus. Bringing the ladders Joseph mounted on the shorter one that was placed in front, while Nicodemus ascended the longer one behind. Joseph had with him a roll of linen so long that after putting it around the body of Jesus, the ends hanging over the cross reached to the ground, where they were held by Simon of Bethany and Lazarus. Then, after taking off the crown of thorns Nicodemus took the pincers and began to pull out the nails from the hands of Jesus and bent the stiffening arms lovingly away from the cross. While they were thus engaged the Magdalen and Mary talked together. "At last," said Mary Magdalene, "the madmen have departed. Be comforted, beloved mother, now we are alone with our friends; the mockery and blasphemy are past and a holy evening stillness surrounds us."

Mary said, "O, my friends! What my Jesus suffered this mother's heart suffered with him. Now he has finished his work and entered into the rest of his Father. Peace also and trust from Heaven fills my soul."

Mary Magdalene comforted her, saying, "He is not taken from us forever; that he promised."

"O, noble men," said Mary to Joseph and Nicodemus, "make haste and bring me the body of my beloved son."

The Magdalene said, "Mother, wilt thou not rest a little here, while we prepare his resting place?" Then seating herself on a stone a little to the right of the cross, Mary waited while her friends made ready to receive the body of Jesus.

"Come, my companions," said Salome, "and help me to prepare the winding sheet to receive the body." They spread the linen on the ground at Mary's feet, placing one end upon her lap.

By this time Nicodemus had extracted the second nail which was in his left hand, and Joseph had taken the nail from the feet of Jesus. Then Simon and Lazarus, holding the ends of the linen roll, slowly lowered the body into the arms of Joseph of Arimathea.

"O, come," said Joseph, "thou sweet and holy burden; let me take thee upon my shoulders." Then with the body of Jesus resting upon his shoulders Joseph began to descend the ladder.

Nicodemus had already come down and awaited him at the foot of the cross. Spreading out his arms to receive the body of Jesus, he said, "Come thou holy body of my only friend, let me embrace thee." Then they carried the body of Jesus and placed it on the linen winding sheet that was prepared for it on his mother's lap. Nicodemus, looking at his wounds sighed, "How the rage of thy enemies hath torn thy flesh."

"Now," said John, "the best of sons rests once more on the bosom of the best of mothers."

Mary looked down upon the pale, blood-spotted face of Jesus, and then sighing heavily she said, "O, my Son, how is thy body covered with wounds!"

"Mother," said John, "from these wounds flowed salvation and blessing for mankind."

"See, mother," said the Magdalene, who stood on her right hand, "how the peace of heaven rests in death upon his face."

Then said Nicodemus who had brought some ointment, "Let us anoint him and then wrap him in this new linen." He then poured the ointment into all the wounds on the body of Jesus.

"He shall be laid," said Joseph of Arimathea, "in my new grave which I have prepared in the rock in my garden."

But before they could wrap him in the winding sheets, Salome came near, and kneeling, raised to her lips the pierced left hand of Jesus saying, "O, best of Masters! One more loving tear upon thy lifeless body."

Then came the Magdalene on the right hand, and kneeling down, stooped low and kissed the right hand, saying, "O, let me once more kiss the hand which has so often blessed me."

Then said John, "We shall see him again."

"Help me," said Joseph to Nicodemus, "to bear him into the garden."

"Blessed am I," said Nicodemus, "that I may lay to rest the remains of him who was sent from God." Then taking up the body they bore it away.

Then said John to Mary and the other woman, "Let us follow the dear, the divine friend."

"It is the last honor," said Mary, "that I can do my Jesus."

On the morning of the third day since Jesus had been crucified, before the sun had arisen, the four soldiers who were appointed to watch the grave sat outside the tomb where the body of Jesus had been laid. One of them awaking, cried, "Brothers, is not the night nearly over?" Then said Titus, "The sky is already reddening in the east; a beautiful spring day is beginning to dawn."

Hardly had he said these words when there was a great earthquake. Pedius springing up exclaimed, "Immortal Gods! What a fearful shock!" "The earth is splitting," cried Rufus. Then there was a peal of thunder. Titus called out, "Away from the rock; it is tottering; it is falling!" and the stone which had been rolled up into the mouth of the sepulcher fell down with a crash.

Jesus arose. For a moment he appeared at the mouth of the sepulchre, radiant in white apparel, while the watch fell on their faces to the ground crying out, "Ye gods, what do we see? A fire from heaven is blinding our eyes!"

Jesus then passed out through the door of the sepulchre and went down into the garden and out of sight.

After awhile the soldiers, who were lying prostrate on the ground said to each other, "Brother, what has happened to us?" Then said one of the soldiers, "I will not stop here another moment."

But Titus looking up said, "The apparition is vanished," and grasping his spear he rose to his feet saying, "Brothers, take heart; we have nothing to fear, as we have done no wrong." They then stood up and saw the open door of the sepulchre from which the stone had fallen. Then said Titus, "The stone is rolled away from the grave. The grave is open."

"Yes," said another, "and the garden door is bolted." Then they went with fear and trembling to the door of the sepulchre, and one looking in, said, "I do not see the corpse."

Then another going farther inside said, "Here is the linen cloth lying in which the body was wrapped. He has gone out of the grave."

Titus said, "He must have risen again, as no one came into the garden."

Then said the third soldier, "It has happened thus as the priests feared."

And Titus answered, "He has fulfilled his word!" "Now, what shall we do?" said the soldiers.

"There is nothing else to be done," said one, "excepting to hasten to the Pharisees and tell them what has happened."

All replied at once, "That we will," and they hastened away.

CHAPTER X

CONCLUSION

I

THE STORY THAT TRANSFORMED THE WORLD

Written by Mr. Stead at Ober-Ammergau the night after witnessing the performance of the Passion Play.

This is the story that transformed the world!

This is the story that transformed the world!

Yes, and will yet transform it!

Yes, thank God, so the answer comes; and will yet transform it until the kingdom comes!

This is the story that transformed the world. I awoke shortly after midnight, after seeing the Passion Play at Ober-Ammergau, with these words floating backward and forward in my head like a peal of bells from some distant spire. Backward and forward they went and came, and came and went.

This is the story that transformed the world!

This is the story that transformed the world. And then in the midst of the reiterated monotone of this insistent message came the glad response from I know not where, "Yes, and will yet transform it!" And then the two met and mingled, strophe and anti-strophe, one answering the other, "This is the story that transformed the world. Yes, and will yet transform the world!"

I tried to sleep, but could not. It was as if church bells were pealing their sweet but imperious music within my brain. So I got up and wrote.

All is silent save the ticking of the watch by my bedside; silent as the stars which gleam down from the blue sky above the cross-crowned crag, which stands like some giant sentinel keeping watch over the village, at its foot. Herod, our host, sleeps soundly, and Johannes, wearied by his double service of waiter at the hotel and his role in the sacred play, is oblivious of all. The crowded thousands who watched for hours yesterday the unfolding of the passion of Christ Jesus of Galilee have disappeared, and I am alone.

But not alone. For as real and as vivid as that same crowd of yesterday seem to me the thronging memories of other days, of the centuries that rise between the time when Jesus really lived on earth, and today. Nineteen hundred years have gone since all that we saw represented yesterday was no mere mimic show but deadly tragic fact; nineteen hundred years during which the shaping power of the world has been that story. The old, old, story never before so vividly realized in all its human significance and its Divine import.

Its human significance, for thank God, we have at last seen Jesus as a man among men, a human being with no halo round his brow, no radiance not of this world marking him off apart from the rest of his fellow-men, but simply Jesus, the Galilean, gibbeted on the gallows of his time, side by side with the scum of mankind.

And it was this story that transformed the world. "Thou hast conquered, O pale Galilean!" Over how many tribes and nations and kindreds of men?

Oh, the wonder of it all, the miracle of miracles surely is this. That this story should have transformed the world. For after all, what was the passion? Looked at as we looked at it yesterday, not from the standpoint of those who see the sacred story through the vista of centuries that have risen in splendor and set in the glory of the cross, but from the standpoint which the actors on the stage assumed yesterday, what was the passion? It was merely a passing episode in the unceasing martyrdom of man. Think you that of the thirty thousand Jews whom the humane Titus by a mere stroke of his stylus condemned to be crucified round the walls of Jerusalem forty years after that scene on Calvary, none suffered like this! For them, also, was reared the horrid cross, nor were they spared the mockings and the scourgings, the cruel thirst, and the slow-drawn agony of days of death. And among all that unnamed multitude how few were there but had some distracted mother to mourn for him, some agonized mother to swoon at the news of his death? Jews they were, as was he. Hero souls, no doubt faithful unto death, and now, let us hope, wearing a crown of life; patriots who knew how to die in the service of the land which their fathers had received from God, and of the temple in which was preserved his holy law. But their self-sacrifice availed not even to save their names from oblivion. Their martyrdom was as powerless to avert the doom of the chosen people as the bursting of the foam-flakes on the sand is to arrest the rush of the returning tide.

Why, then, should the death of one Jew have transformed the world, while the death of these uncounted thousands failed even to save the synagogue?

Why? That is the question that the Passion Play forces home—a question which never even comes to the mind of those who are accustomed from childhood to regard this Jew as mysteriously Divine, not so much man as God, cut off from us and our daily littleness by the immeasurable abyss that yawns between the finite and the infinite. This greatest of all the miracles, the coming of Christendom into being, has become so much a matter of course that we marvel as little at it as we do at the sunrise—which also in its way is a wonder worthy enough. Think for a moment of the many myriads of fierce heathen, worshipping all manner of proud ancestral gods, that have gone down before the might of that pale form. Civilizations and empires have gone down into the void; darkness covers them over and oblivion is fast erasing the very inscriptions which history has traced on their tombs. But the kingdom which this man founded knoweth no end. The voice that echoed from the hills of Galilee is echoing today from hills the Romans never trod, and the story of that life is rendered in tongues unknown at Pentecost. The more you look at it from the standpoint of the contemporaries of the carpenter of Nazareth the more incredibly marvelous it appears.

And this is the great gain of the Passion Play. It takes us clear back across the ages to the standpoint of those who saw Jesus, the Galilean, as merely a man among men. It compels us to see him without the aureole of Divinity, as he appeared to those who knew him from his boyhood, and who said, "Are not his brethren still with us?" It is true that it is still not real enough. The dresses are too beautiful—everything is conventional. We have here not the real Christ, the Jew, the outcast and the vagabond. For him we must wait till Vereschagin or some other realist painter may bring us reality. But even behind all the despisers of conventional Christian art, we have at least a sufficiently human figure to elicit sympathy, compassion and love. We get near enough to Christ to hear the blows that fall upon his face, to appreciate the superior respectability of the high priests, and to understand the contempt of Herod for the "king of fools." Not until we start low enough do we understand the heights to which the crucified has risen. It is only after realizing the depths of his humiliation we can even begin to understand the miracle of the transformation that he has wrought.

Nor is that all. It is the greatest thing, but it does not stand alone. For besides enabling us to realize the story which transformed the world, it enables us to understand the agency by which that story effected its beneficent revolution.

I learned more of the inner secret of the Catholic church in Ober-Ammergau than ever I learnt in Rome. Yet there is nothing distinctively Roman about the Passion Play. With the exception of the legend of St. Veronica with which Gabriel Maxs' picture has familiarized every Protestant who looks into a photograph shop and sees the strange face on the handkerchief, whose eyes reveal themselves beneath your gaze, there is nothing from first to last to which the Protestant Alliance could take exception. And yet it is all there. There, condensed into eight hours or less, is the whole stock-in-trade of the Christian church. It was in its effort to impress that story upon the heart of man that there came into being all that is distinctively Roman. To teach truth by symbols, to speak through the eye as much as the ear, to leave no gate of approach unsummoned by the bearer of the glad tidings of great joy, and above all in so doing to use every human element of pathos, of tragedy, and of awe that can touch the heart or impress the imagination—that was the mission of the church; and as it got further and further afield and had to deal with rude and ruder barbarians the tendency grew to print in still larger capitals. The Catholic church, in short, did for religion what the new journalism has done for the press. It has sensationalized in order to get a hearing among the masses.

Protestantism that confines its gaze solely to the sublime central figure of the gospel story walks with averted face past the beautiful group of the holy women. Because others have ignorantly worshiped, therefore we must not even contemplate. But plant a competent Protestant dramatic critic in the theater of Ober-Ammergau, let him look with dry eyes if he can upon the leave-taking at Bethany, and then as the universal sob rises from thousands of gazers, he will realize perhaps for the first time how intense is the passion of sympathy which they have sealed up, how powerful the emotion to which they are forbidden to appeal. The most pathetic figure in the Passion Play is not Christ, but his mother. There is in him also sublimity. She is purely pathetic. And after Mary the mother comes Mary Magdalene. Protestantism will have much leeway to make up before it can find any influence so potent for softening the hearts and inspiring the imagination of men. Even in spite of all the obloquy of centuries of superstition, and of the consequent centuries of angry reaction against this abuse, these two women stand out against the gloom of the past radiant as the angels of God, and yet the true ideals of the womanhood of the world.

Yes, this was the story that transformed the world! This and no other. This it was which to make visible, men carved it in stone and built it in the cathedral, and then, lest even the light of heaven should come to the eye of man without bearing with it the story of the cross, they filled their church windows with stained glass, so that the sun should not shine without throwing into brighter relief the leading features of the wonder-working epoch of his life and death. Wherever you go in Christendom you come upon endless reproductions of the scenes which yesterday we saw presented with all the vividness of the drama. The cross, the nails, the lance, have been built into the architecture of the world, often by the descendants of the men who crucified their Redeemer—not knowing what they did. For centuries art was but an endless repetition in color or in stone of the scenes we witnessed yesterday, or of incidents in lives which had been transformed by these scenes. The more utterly we strip the story of the Passion of all supernatural significance the more irresistibly comes back upon the mind the overwhelming significance of the transformation which it has affected in the world.

Why?—I keep asking why? If there were no divine and therefore natural law behind all that, why should that trivial incident, the crucifixion of one among the unnumbered host of vagabonds executed every year in the reign of Tiberius and the Caesars that followed him, how comes it that we are here today? Why are railways built and special trains organized and six thousand people gathered in curiosity or in awe to see the representation of this simple tale? How comes it if there were no dynamo at the other end of that long coil of centuries, that the light should still be shining at our end today? Shining alas! not so brightly as could be wished, but to shine at all, is that in itself not miraculous?

Through all the ages it has shone with varying luster. And still it shines. The dawn of a new day as I write is breaking upon this mountain valley. The cocks are crowing in the village, recalling the apostle who in the midst of the threatening soldiery denied his Lord. And even as Peter went out and wept bitterly, and ever after became the stoutest and bravest disciple of the Master, may it not yet be with those of this generation who also have denied their Redeemer?

Who knows? The transformation would be far less startling than that which converted the Coliseum from the shambles of imperial Rome into the gigantic monument of triumphant martyrdom, far less violent than that which made the German forbears of these good Ammergauers into Christian folk.

But if the transformation is to be effected, and the light and warmth of a new day of faith, and hope, and love, are to irradiate the world, then may it not be confidently asserted that in the old, old story of the cross lies the secret of the only power which can save mankind?

II

THE INTERPRETATION OF THE STORY

Wherein does it modify orthodox opinions? Chiefly in humanizing them, in making the gospel story "palpitate with actuality" to quote the French phrase which Matthew Arnold loved to use. These people on the stage at Ober-Ammergau are not lay figures, mere abstract representations of the virtues or the opposite. They live, breathe and act just as if they were actors in a French or Russian novel. That is the great difference. These poor players have brought our Lord to life again. In their hands he is no mere influence of abstraction, no infinite and almighty ruler of the universe. He may be and no doubt every one of the Ober-Ammergauers would shrink with horror from the suggestion that he was any other than the second person of the trinity. But they have done more than repeat the Athanasian creed. They have shown how it came to be believable. If that poor carpenter's son by getting himself crucified as one part fool and three parts seditious adventurer could revolutionize the world, then the inference seemed irresistible that he must have been divine. If the illegitimate son of a Bengalese peasant hanged by order of our lieutenant-governor in the northwest provinces because of the mischief he was making among the Moslems of Lahore were to establish his faith on the ruins of Westminster Abbey, and install the successor of his leading disciple on the throne of the British empire, we should not wonder at his apotheosis. To do so much, with so little material, compels the inference that there is the infinite behind. Nothing but a God could control such a machine. It needed a fulcrum in eternity to make such a change in the things of time with so weak a lever as the life of this Galilean.

But it is not only Christ himself who becomes real to us, but what is almost as important, we see his contemporaries as they saw themselves, or as he saw them. Caiaphas—who that has seen Burgomaster Lang in that leading role can feel anything but admiration and sympathy for the worthy chief of the Sanhedrin? He had everything on his side to justify him. Law, respectability, patriotism, religious expediency, common sense. Against him there was only this poor vagabond from Nazareth—and the Invisible. But Caiaphas, like other men, does not see the Invisible and he acts, according to his lights, as he was bound to act. He is the great prototype of the domineering and intolerant ecclesiastic all the world over. Since the crucifixion he has often changed his clothes. But at heart he is the same. He has worn the three-crowned hat of the successor of Peter; he has paraded in a bishop's miter; he has often worn the gown and bands of Presbyterian Geneva. Caiaphas is eternal. He produces himself in every church and in every village, because there is a latent Caiaphas in every heart.

Perhaps the character who comes out best is Pilate. He is a noble Roman, whose impartiality and rectitude, coupled with an anxious desire to take the line of least resistance and find out some practical middle course, is worthy of that imperial race to whose vices, as well as to many of their virtues, we English have succeeded. Pilate did his best to save Jesus up to a point—beyond that point he did not go, and according to the accepted ethics of men in his position, it would have been madness to have gone. Why should he, Pontius Pilate, procurator of Judea, risk his career and endanger the tranquillity of Jerusalem merely to save a poor wretch like that Galilean? What Englishman who has ever ruled a province in India, where religious ferment was rife, who would not have felt tempted to act as Pilate acted—nay, would not have acted as he acted without even the hesitation he showed, if the life of some poor devil of a wandering fakir stood between him and the peace of the empire? Would to God that British magistrates, even at home in our own land, would give the despised and unpopular poor man the same number of chances Pilate gave to Jesus. With Downing street eager for the conviction of a socialist agitator, and the whole of society and the mob savage against him, a man would be a fool who would not appeal from Bow street or old Bailey to so just a judge as Pilate. To the last Pilate never made himself the willing instrument of popular frenzy. He argued against it, he denounced it, he resorted to every subterfuge by which he could save the prisoner's life, and it was only when the Sanhedrin threatened to denounce him to Caesar as an enemy of the emperor that he unwillingly gave way. Here and there no doubt there are among our latter day magistrates and judges fanatical believers in abstract right, who would have risked the empire rather than let a hair of Christ's head be touched; but the average English or American magistrate—especially if the accused was "only a nigger"—would shrug his shoulders at such Quixotism as folly and worse. It is better, they would say, that one man should die, even unjustly, than that everything should be upset.

Another person who comes out better than might be expected is Judas. The conception of his character is very fine and very human. Judas, as the treasurer of the little band, naturally felt indignant at the apparent wanton extravagance which led Mary Magdalene to pour ointment worth 300 pence upon the head of her master. There is real human nature and sound practical common sense in his reply to those who told him not to worry about the money, when he retorted, "Who is there to take care about it if I don't?" Judas never really from first to last meditates betraying his master to death. The salves which he lays to his conscience when consenting to identify Jesus at night are very ingenious. Judas was a smart man who calculated he stood to win in any event. He got the indispensable cash; all that he did was to indicate what could perfectly well have been discovered without his aid; if Jesus were what he believed him to be he could easily have baffled his enemies; if he were not, well, then, he had deceived them. But the moment Judas learns that he has really endangered his master's life, his whole demeanor changes. He flings back the blood money at the feet of those who had given it to him, and in the madness of despair he hangs himself. So far from Judas being callous to Christ's fate, his suicide was a proof that his penitence was far more agonizing than that of Peter.

Simon Peter also comes in for a share in the general rehabilitation.

It was impossible not to feel sympathy for the hasty old man, hustled from side to side by a pack of violent soldiery. Knowing moreover that he had cut off one of their ears but a few hours before, and that if they recognized him his own ears would have been cropped, even if he didn't share the fate of the crucified, his denial is so natural under the circumstances that you cease to marvel that even the cock crow on the roof failed to remind him of his master's warning.

The Passion Play has at least done this—it sets us discussing the conduct of Caiaphas and Pilate and Judas, as if they were our contemporaries, as if they were statesmen at Westminster or at Washington or administrators in India or Canada. And this, no doubt, is no small service, for these men are types of human character who are eternally re-embodied among us.

III

THE RELIGION OF THE FUTURE

The story of the Passion Play has ever been real to me in another than a Catholic sense. It has been the perpetual re-incarnation of the divine story in the history of our own times that has absorbed my attention. These ancient figures on the stage of New Testament history were but of importance in so far as they lived again in our own life. Of their mystical theological significance I am, of course, not speaking. This is a thing apart. But the perpetual re-incarnation of God's Messiah in the great causes of justice, freedom and humanity, it is that which has made the gospel story ever new to me.

Leaving Ober-Ammergau I returned by Switzerland to London. At Lucerne while waiting for the train, I turned over the book in the waiting-room that describes the construction of the Gotthard railway. About one thousand tons of dynamite, it is said, had sufficed to pierce the tunnels through the mountain barrier that separated Italy from Switzerland. Blasting powder could never have done the work. That helped to level the military roads for the legions of Suwarrow. It needed dynamite to tunnel the St. Gotthard—dynamite directed by science—and as I read this I fell a-thinking. The old story, that mediaeval Christ in magenta and pearl gray, with his disciples in artistic symphonies of harmonious and contrasted color, no doubt transformed the world. But a new world has arisen which sorely needs transforming again, and is it not possible that the conventional Christ, who no doubt did mighty things in the past, may have become as obsolete as blasting powder. May we not hope that if the conventional Christ did so much, the real Christ may do much more; that the realization of the Christ as he actually lived and died among us may be as much superior in its transforming efficacy as the dynamite of the modern engineer is to the powder sack of the soldiers who marched under old Suwarrow? Of one thing we may at least be certain, and that is, if everyone of those who call themselves by the Christian name would but say one Christ-like word, and do one Christ-like deed between every sunrise and sunset, it would lift a very Alpine mass of sorrow and anxiety from the weary heart of the world. What then might not be done if in very truth, and with all sincerity, we, each of us, tried to be a real Christ in his or her sphere, the sent of God in the midst of those with whom we pass our lives?

One more word and I have done. The actors play different parts as they grow old. They begin with being children in the tableaux and they pass in turn from one role to another. The Judas of 1890 was the apostle John in 1880. When the Christ was selected in 1870, he was chosen out of four competitors. One of the unsuccessful today plays King Herod, the other Pontius Pilate. So it is ever in real life. Few, indeed, are those who are always Christs. When Christians ceased to be martyrs they martyred their enemies. The church came from the catacombs to establish the inquisition. In our own lives we may be Christs today and atheists tomorrow. Power and authority destroy more Christs than the dungeon and the stake. And perhaps one reason why the Ober-Ammergauers have been able to give us the Christ we see this year is because in their secluded valley they have remained poor and humble in spirit, and have never ceased to remember the story that transformed the world.

www.ingramcontent.com/pod-product-compliance
Lightning Source LLC
Chambersburg PA
CBHW011255040426
42453CB00015B/2416